T0076633

The Code of Honor

The Code of Honor

Embracing Ethics in Cybersecurity

Paul J. Maurer
Ed Skoudis

WILEY

Contents

Introduction: "Like Your Hair Is On Fire"

*"The Chinese use two brush strokes to write the word 'crisis.'
One brush stroke stands for danger, the other for opportunity.
In a crisis, be aware of the danger—but recognize the
opportunity."*

– President John F. Kennedy

Dear Reader,

You may not realize it yet, but we would like to humbly suggest to you that, metaphorically speaking, your hair is on fire—or at least you should be responding to the current state of the cybersecurity industry and its impact on the world with an alarmed sense of immediate concern. We assume you have opened these pages because you are a leader with cybersecurity responsibilities, a cybersecurity practitioner, or a student preparing for a role in this industry. Or, although you may have another role, perhaps cybersecurity is quickly becoming a critical concern in your daily work. Regardless of what brought you here, we are quite sure the challenges we address in these pages are more far-reaching and urgent than you may even realize right now.

The Code of Honor is the result of a journey we began several years ago to address an expanding ethical vacuum in our industry, where critical decisions are often made without regard to their ethical implications. At the same time, the weight and financial impact of our decision-making is rapidly increasing. As you will learn in the coming pages, the crossroads of cybersecurity and ethics aren't some philosophical "pie in the sky" discussion. Cybersecurity professionals hold a great deal of power and enormous levels of responsibility in the workplace and the broader economy. It is a high-pressure, fast-paced, and exciting field where ethical decision-making can make the difference between success and abject disaster, not only for your career but for your organization, customers, or constituents, and perhaps far beyond. The topics we explore in this book are integral to the daily operations of nearly every industry and are essential to the very stability of our modern world.

As the cybersecurity industry is changing at light speed, we must truly respond to the emergent ethical challenges with a level of "hair on fire" determination and precision. Our offering in *The Code of Honor* is a systematic and thoughtfully constructed program for building best practices regarding ethics in decision-making in the tech industry with a specific focus on cybersecurity. This book presents a concise, carefully designed, and timeless set of ethics that will engage everyone from C-suite leaders who work on the periphery of the cyber world to the most seasoned cybersecurity professionals and everyone in between.

We thought it best to begin by answering a few questions that will help you maximize your experience and effectively engage with the pages ahead.

How Should You Read This Book?

To craft this book, we spent a year thinking through and documenting various ethical dilemmas we've seen in the cybersecurity industry in our several decades, worth of experience as practitioners, leaders, and educators. From those discussions, we spent a great deal of time wrestling with each other to formulate a clear, short, valuable Cybersecurity Code of Honor to provide a framework for ethical decision-making for real-world cybersecurity leaders and practitioners. We then refined the code of honor by gathering input from dozens of friends and colleagues throughout the cybersecurity industry. We wrote this book to provide an in-depth tool that expands on the ideas of that code of honor, which is in Appendix A of the book.

The chapters are written in a specific sequence and are meant to be read in order. Every chapter supports a tenant of the code of honor. Each chapter is full of engaging stories, industry-specific illustrations, and practical, real-world applications designed to teach the essential foundational concepts behind this widely accepted code of ethics that is becoming an industry standard. The book is designed to be read individually or in a team or corporate setting. We highly encourage you to work through the lessons of each chapter with other professionals who can help you learn and grow.

Why Are There Two Authors but Only One Voice?

While "we" (Paul and Ed) contributed equally significantly to this product, we did not want to confuse the reader by writing with two different voices throughout these chapters. We chose to approach the important concepts in this book with one consistent voice to make the reading experience straightforward and ensure the content is front and center. On rare occasions, we will refer to specific experiences of Paul or Ed by name, but we will generally refer to our common and shared experiences as "we."

How Should You Approach the Critical Applications Case Studies?

Every chapter closes with a case study called "Critical Applications," designed to help you utilize the essential skills and concepts you have learned in that chapter and those before it. These case studies are meant to challenge you to consider the ethical implications of the choices we must make in our professional lives. While the names, companies, and details of these stories have been changed, they are based on real-world examples from across our industry that we have observed or advised our colleagues about.

Each case study can be used to facilitate lively small group discussion and debate in classrooms, corporate sessions, training exercises, or seminar settings. Not only are these studies powerful teaching tools for students and industry professionals, but they can also assist C-suite leaders who need to better understand the scope of cybersecurity challenges, define their liability and responsibility, and think strategically about budget and hiring personnel necessary to protect their organizations. As you'll see later in this book, we think of cybersecurity ethical practices rather like muscles—the more you work them out, the stronger you'll get. Please use these "Critical Applications" scenarios at the end of each chapter as an exercise regimen for yourself and your team.

How Should You Use the Cybersecurity Code of Honor?

Our book closes with the Cybersecurity Code of Honor that is a singular universal code of ethics currently being adopted by cybersecurity practitioners and leaders around the world. The Cybersecurity Code of Honor was born out of research, interviews, and conversations with the world's leading experts in our field and can be applied to a wide range of ethical decisions you may confront in the cybersecurity industry. We recognize that various cybersecurity certification bodies and other related organizations have developed oaths and codes of honor for holders of those certs. We applaud their efforts and have reviewed each of them carefully as we formulated the Cybersecurity Code of Honor. We aim to build something applicable beyond individual cybersecurity certifications and even individual job roles—to create something useful as a framework throughout the cybersecurity world.

We have been humbled to witness the immediate impact the Cybersecurity Code of Honor has made across the industry. It is our hope it will also be adopted by you, your organization, or your school to help provide a singular lens through which best ethical practices in our field may be determined.

A Challenge to Make the World a Better Place

We have done our best to present the lessons about this system of cybersecurity ethics in a way that will engage everyone. It is our sincerest hope that this book can function as a comprehensive learning tool for students, cybersecurity professionals, and business leaders who have been desperately seeking a widely agreed-upon set of principles to guide their professional and personal ethical decisions. We believe that this book (and its corresponding code of honor) can be a catalyst for your career advancement, help enhance the security of your organization, and even fast-track your leadership teams' success. Ultimately, we challenge you to embrace the ethical standards and practices in this book for the world's greater good.

Sincerely,
Paul and Ed

CHAPTER

1

One Code to Rule Them All?

"The most important human endeavor is the striving for morality in our actions. Our inner balance and even our very existence depend on it. Only morality in our actions can give beauty and dignity to life."

– Albert Einstein

"The time is always right to do what is right."

– Dr. Martin Luther King Jr.

Cybercrime and cybersecurity should be among the foremost concerns of every industry, service, and every civic interest. Why? Cyber technology effectively runs the modern world from banking to healthcare, retail to sanitation, and governance to modern warfare. Cybersecurity practitioners wield great power, are under intense pressure, work in a culture that is changing at warp speed, and often have profound responsibilities. The fast-paced environment of our industry can be a breeding ground for mistakes, misused authority, and even intentionally abused power. The unprecedented speed of innovation in the 21st century has left us without a clear system of ethics for this great economic and security threat of our age. We would be remiss if we didn't begin by sharing some statistics with you reflecting how cybersecurity and cybercrime impact the world as we write this book. While the numbers may read like an archeological time capsule by the time you read them, it is our way of pulling the "fire alarm" in the midst of an unfolding global crisis.

- According to research, an estimated 53.35 million U.S. citizens were affected by cybercrime just in the first half of 2022.[1]

- Ransomware attacks in 2022 cost global businesses an estimated $20 billion. As cybercriminals are becoming rapidly more advanced and targeting businesses that can pay higher ransom fees, experts believe that $20 billion will balloon to more than $30 billion just in the next year.[2]

- The average cost to an individual organization that has suffered a data breach in 2022 was $4.35 million.[3]

- This cyber arms race by the world's bad actors is also leading to increased security spending. According to a recent report, cybersecurity spending is expected to reach $172 billion by the close of 2022.

Every time we open our browser or news app to check the latest research, the proverbial fire presents its rapid spread in the news cycle of the day. Today's headline points out that "Crypto-hackers steal $3 Billion This Year," while another proclaims, "2025 will be the biggest year for Digital Heists!" Cyberattackers, through ransomware and other insidious schemes, have caused massive damage to banks, hospitals, schools, critical infrastructures, and more. And it seems to be only getting worse.

In Case You Are Wondering Why You Should Care

For those of you on the periphery of our industry or simply new to the job, it is important to know what you are risking if you choose to ignore this cybersecurity crisis (no matter how big or small your organization is). Even today, there are too many leaders who still don't fully understand the scope of impact that cyberattacks can have in our world. Here are just a few of the effects that cyberattacks can inflict upon you and your business:

- You may suffer damage to your computer systems. When malicious computer attackers target your business, they can damage or destroy data on those systems, and the cost to repair or rebuild them can be extremely high.

- Attackers can steal sensitive data from your business such as consumer information or even trade secrets, which can have a dramatic impact on your company's reputation and financial standing.

- A cyberattack can interrupt the services that your business provides and cause you to lose money, customers, and time.

- You can face legal consequences from a cyberattack. You and your business can be held accountable for damages to consumers.

- Being hit by a cyberattack can ruin your brand and your reputation, making it harder to attract and keep customers. It can negatively impact your business long after the immediate damages of an attack have been corrected.

- Finally, there is always cybercrime and identify theft's impact on real people. If cybercriminals steal consumer information from your systems, those customers will be put at risk, affecting your consumer retention, impacting stakeholder trust, and resulting in legal issues. Even more concerning are cyberattacks that break into healthcare systems, transportation, or other critical infrastructures, perhaps causing severe damage to life and limb.

Cybersecurity is no longer an issue that you can ignore. We would argue that your success as a business, a professional, and a leader could be tied to how seriously you address this problem. Experts are currently predicting that cybercrime will eclipse the gross domestic product (GDP) of the world's largest economies in the near future. While it may sound fantastical, we are here to tell you it is a stark and unnerving reality.

It's as if we are trying to put out this worldwide four-alarm fire with a water gun. Every day in the cybersecurity industry, we are fighting for the resources, staffing, education, and ethical framework to keep attackers at bay. While the global workforce in our industry stands at around 4.7 million workers, it is predicted that there will be an astounding 3.4 million cybersecurity worker *shortage* worldwide within a few years. Currently, we need 600,000 positions filled in the United States *alone*. As we struggle to keep up with the demand to fill positions, we also must be vigilant to find good candidates of reputable character who are committed to serving the greater good. If we fill open positions with people who lack the ethical framework and character to put it into real-world practice, we'll only make the problem worse—*much* worse.

This is a problem that touches the day-to-day operations of nearly every public and private entity. Yes, by the time you read these words, the numbers will be outdated, and unfortunately, the challenges will be way bigger. There is simply no evidence that these trends will reverse course in the near future. Technology will continue to dominate the business landscape and become ever more a part of all of life. We are not going to go backward from our online, on-demand, virtual world any time soon. And of course, we are not likely going to become less technologically advanced or cyber-integrated. Attackers are not going to give up. Cybercrime is too lucrative an industry.

Is there a way to stop or at least slow down the trend? Is there any hope?

Do We Need Ethics in Cybersecurity?

Yes. An ethical standard in cybersecurity is fundamental to its future. If you work in cybersecurity, your day-to-day job can feel like fighting fires. Your day can go from 0 to 100 with one email or intrusion alert, and you will often find yourself in high-stress situations that have serious consequences on your company and its customers or stakeholders. One of the realities of working in fast-paced, pressure-filled environments is the ever-present temptation to cut corners or take shortcuts. There is tremendous pressure on both practitioners and leadership in our line of work to make the *right* decisions because those choices can have far-reaching impacts on numerous individuals. We can better illustrate a few of the common ethical challenges with a story about two professionals who have been recently affected by cybercrime.

Sarah is the CEO of a midsize medical device engineering company that has been hit recently with a ransomware attack. It isn't long before her small security team identifies the entry point through a third-party IT service provider that is also used by several of her fiercest competitors. As her cybersecurity team rolls into response and investigation, the questions mount: Is the attacker truly connected to the service company, or is it just set up to appear that way? Does the CEO have a responsibility to alert her competitors of the potential breach? Do competitors have an advantage over Sarah during the downtime caused by the attack? Her firm designs medical devices for several healthcare organizations. Are there legal obligations to alert those entities of the attack? Do they have to alert their parent company, who could be negatively affected by this event if it went public? When the attackers reach out with a ransom, should they quietly pay to make the entire situation go away? Is that even possible? How do they balance an obligation to protect the public and their obligation to defend the interests of their engineering firm? Is there an ethical framework by which all of these complicated questions could be examined and answered properly?

Jim is a security operations center (SOC) analyst at the very company servicing all of those medical device engineering firms with IT support. He was recently asked to do some lucrative after-hours security consulting at a local company. While that freelance work technically conflicted with the noncompete clause he signed in his contract with his primary employer, Jim accepted it because he really needs the money. And the chief information security officer (CISO) of his organization didn't seem to mind that he was doing this side gig, although she never actually approved of it. Jim has recently learned that his company was breached and that his CISO has chosen not to share information about the breach with her superiors, shareholders, or customers. The organization has policies and procedures that his boss is simply not following. Because he is a lead analyst, he has all the data he needs concerning the breach and its impact to go over his CISO's head and warn the company president. He has also learned that the breach is likely connected to the ransomware attack on several of the engineering firms his company services (like Sarah's). Attackers are leveraging his company's access to customer environments to deploy ransomware. But, Jim is nervous that his lucrative side gig could be exposed by his CISO as retribution if he chooses to speak up about the breach. What has Jim gotten himself into? Does he have an ethical obligation to tell someone about the breach? Is he miscalculating the level of concern about the breach? Does he really have the full picture of how his CISO is responding to the crisis? One thing is true: Jim has no idea the significant impact his personal choices could have on Sarah and other engineering firms his company supports!

For those of you who are industry professionals, Sarah's and Jim's stories may seem common. If you are a C-suite leader on the periphery of cybersecurity, you should know that situations such as this occur every day. These are stories of well-respected professionals, not criminals. But, as we connect the question of ethics to cybersecurity work, it is important to recognize that many of the attacks your organization may face are the result of an insider threat, meaning they are too often a consequence of either a negligent, confused, or malicious employee. According to some research, malicious insiders are responsible for around 22% of security incidents. Stanford University, working with a top cybersecurity organization, recently found that nearly 88% of data breaches are caused by an *employee mistake* or mishandling of a situation. We have been around the industry long enough to see that many of these mistakes are simply lapses in judgment that could be avoided! In this business, our daily decision-making matters.

The reality is that cybersecurity, behind all the screens, programs, systems, and hardware, is still a human business. Real people are making real decisions, and those decisions need a reference point, a guide, or a compass. Now, you may be wondering if there are already ethical and moral codes used at all in the cybersecurity field. The short answer is yes, there are various ethical codes of honor in the industry. Many are very specific and are associated with various industry technical certifications. We appreciate and support those efforts to drive ethical behaviors in conjunction with technical excellence. However, these efforts tend to be disjointed and bound to a specific technical expertise rather than the industry at large. Most of all, they are usually a series of required behaviors and proscribed activities, but none of them is truly an ethical framework for decision-making. There has never been one universally agreed upon or adopted code for cybersecurity ethics. We believe that there is a tremendous need for a framework to help leaders and practitioners understand and analyze the implications of the decisions they make. A collectively agreed upon code of honor supported by a well-thought-out code of ethics has never been available.

As a result, everyone is left to navigate their own path. Each organization uses its own map, or no map, to navigate the thousands of daily choices that consequently impact thousands (and sometimes millions) of people. We need one direction and one code now more than ever.

Long-Standing Models for the Code

To think through what our Cybersecurity Code of Honor (included in Appendix A of this book and available online) and this book should look like, we examined the merits of the world's universally accepted moral and ethical systems in similarly vital areas of industry, civics, and life. We found that throughout the history of civilization, our greatest modernizations in the most *essential* fields such as law, medicine, and even warfare have always driven us to come together and find a commonly held, universal, and guiding framework for character and ethics.

We believe that the scope and magnitude of cybersecurity is on par with the scope and magnitude of the fields of law, medicine, and warfare. In fact, as you read these words, cybersecurity is redefining warfare and significantly impacting law and medicine. Yet, humans in law, medicine, and warfare have had the benefit of time for two millennia or more to develop the ethical codes and frameworks that guide them in civilized nations. The difference is that cybersecurity is new, and we don't have two millennia to figure this out. It has to happen now, given the rapid pace of technological change, the centrality of information technology, and its security in our daily lives.

One of the oldest guiding documents in history is the Hippocratic oath, still revered and utilized by physicians around the globe. The oath addresses the moral obligations of its oath-takers, including the need "to treat the ill to the best of one's ability, to preserve a patient's privacy, to teach the secrets of medicine to the next generation."[4]

The Geneva Conventions of 1949 and their additional protocols were international treaties adopted after World War II and vital to limiting the barbarity of armed conflict. They were mutually accepted by civilized nations across the world to try to protect people who do not take part in the fighting (such as civilians, medics, and aid workers) and those who can no longer fight (such as the wounded, the sick, or prisoners of war). The Geneva Conventions and protocols are a descendant of "Just War" theory, which can be traced back as far as Ancient Egypt.

We researched various ethical codes across multiple cultures. For example, in the United States, our social workers have one binding set of principles called the National Association of Social Workers (NASW) Code of Ethics that help guide professional practices. Alternatively, lawyers have a binding oath in each U.S. state as well as a single guiding code of ethics through the American Bar Association. Of course, the levels to which these moral agreements have an impact or consequence vary from field to field. Many are voluntary, and most are not enforceable by law, but upholding such codes may determine whether someone is able to maintain their license to practice in their respective fields. We believe these oaths and codes of honor are all vital to providing a singular lens through which to examine professional and personal practices while establishing a gold standard. These universally accepted ethical codes act as a guide in a world where we are so often faced with complicated and confusing choices.

Why the Need for the Code Is Urgent

The pace of development in technology is so rapid, it is nearly impossible to keep up. In cybersecurity, offensive capabilities advance relentlessly, while our defensive postures and infrastructures struggle to stay relevant as they grow mind-bogglingly complex. All the while, the underlying technological infrastructure and frameworks shift at a relentless, and even bewildering, pace. We will continue to detail these challenges throughout the book, but suffice it to say we are in the midst of a great cybersecurity arms race.

The speed with which technology is changing also dictates the pressing need for a way to interpret best practices from an ethical perspective in this shifting landscape. As we advance, we are faced with new questions and challenges about dealing with privacy, intellectual property, individual rights, and our stakeholder protection. Why have a single code to address all of these issues? *Because while the cyber world changes daily, ethics and doing the right thing do not.* Technology is a shifting sea, and a common ethical framework is a lighthouse. Our world is complex, and sometimes we face really difficult decisions. We need a structure to evaluate how to navigate these hard choices.

We set out to write this book because we are overdue for ethical guidance in cybersecurity. The absence of such governance creates mass confusion. It's time to operate by being grounded in something more than "do what feels right." We have functioned too long out of situational ethics, making it up as we go, that in the end, serves no one. Situational ethics are untethered, untrustworthy, and unevenly applied without a universally accepted decision-making framework. We need a better way to navigate the critical choices we are faced with each day in this field.

In recent years, there has been a growing sense of urgency for a defined ethical standard. With the help of the U.S. National Security Agency and numerous cybersecurity industry leaders, we have researched and constructed a code of honor to provide a tool for the greater good.

In J.R.R. Tolkien's *Lord of the Rings* trilogy, you may remember the folklore behind the story that included the many Rings of Power. Different civilizations in Tolkien's intricately designed world had their own set of rings that led to their individual ways of interpreting and operating in the world and their systems of morality. In Tolkien mythology, to control all of these rings, one ring was finally forged. In the stories, it is actually called the "One Ring." It strikes us, by analogy, that this is exactly what the cybersecurity world needs. In a world of disjointed and disconnected ethical codes, "one c," is desperately needed and is what we have attempted to create. It is our hope that this code of honor and book might serve to bind people together with an underlying ethical framework for decision-making.

This book is designed to deepen your understanding of the foundation that allows this code of honor to stand the test of time. Additionally, through stories and case studies, we want to show how to put these ethical principles into practice to help protect your organization, protect the public, and enhance the cybersecurity profession. As thousands of practitioners and leaders have already adopted the Cybersecurity Code of Honor, the value-add has already become apparent in having one consistent ethical code that ties together practitioners across the industry.

Finally, let's step away from the philosophical and cultural ramifications of ethics for just a moment. We hope this discussion is also extremely personal to you. Why? Well, the stark reality is that your professional success and advancement in our industry is a matter of trust, and earning trust is in large measure a product of making consistent ethical choices. In that way, practicing cybersecurity ethics isn't just what is best for the world—it is what is best for you and your professional trajectory. Practicing ethics in the cybersecurity field will be beneficial to your upward mobility. It will positively affect your reputation, support your career advancement, and be tied to the success of your organization or business. Along the way, you may even help make the world a safer, more secure, and more ethical place.

2

This Is a Human Business

"I will treat all people with dignity and respect."
— The Cybersecurity Code of Honor

"It isn't what we say or think that defines us, but
what we do."
— Jane Austen, *Sense and Sensibility*, 1811

"Mankind was my business. The common welfare was my
business.... The dealings of my trade were but a drop of
water in the comprehensive ocean of my business!"
— Charles Dickens, *A Christmas Carol*, 1843

Brady grabbed his backpack and hustled through the
parking garage toward the elevators. He was running
late to get to the office early that Tuesday morning. The line
at the coffee shop had been a little slow, and this was going

to be a triple espresso kind of morning. He briskly moved through the aisle of cubicles from the elevator toward his chair in the cybersecurity department at the regional financial institution's headquarters to find his co-worker Elizabeth in full-blown panic mode. "I saw your text," Brady told his co-worker as they immediately went to work. "Well. It's much worse than we thought yesterday," Elizabeth responded coolly, "I've been fielding nonstop calls since sunrise."

The two security analysts spotted a possible breach the day before and carefully followed their company's incident response procedures. They were certain the problem was contained until the last few hours when it spiraled into a full-blown corporate crisis. Down the hall in the corner office, Kit, the company chief information security officer (CISO), had broken into a cold sweat as she stared out the window talking on the phone to her chief information officer (CIO), Catherine. They had just wrapped up a conference call with the director of the outsourced managed security service provider (MSSP) they hired last quarter to support their internal team. Early assessments estimated the attacker had exfiltrated names, addresses, Social Security numbers, account numbers, and balances of nearly 50,000 customers. Kit and Catherine tried to remain calm on the phone as they reviewed the damage and gathered information to brief everyone on the executive team from the communications director to the chief executive officer (CEO). Catherine lamented to her CISO, "Kit, people are going to lose their jobs over this." Her statement was true. As information filtered through, it was becoming clear that while they had caught the crack at the top of the dam in the breach the night before, they had all missed the real damage being done under the surface where no one was looking. Back in the cubicles, Elizabeth and Brady had already considered their own job security as they hurried to gather reports on the extent of the data breach.

The very same morning, just miles away, in a small apartment, Genevieve, an elderly and retired widow on a fixed income, answered an unusual morning phone call and began answering questions from a stranger who claimed to work for the bank and knew her Social Security and account numbers. The caller explained that he needed the login information for her online banking to correct an error, or her account would be frozen. She was flustered but thankful for his "helpful attitude," so she faithfully gave him all the information he needed, hoping to help solve the problem but never realizing he was a scammer connected to the breach.

Of course, Genevieve's caller would go on to use that information to transfer $10,000 from her retirement account, causing significant financial hardship. In just a few short days, Kit, the CISO, would be asked to resign by the bank's leadership and board of directors. The MSSP would lose their contract and be blamed publicly for not identifying the breach early enough. Genevieve and hundreds of other consumers including moms, dads, college students, and retirees would lose money (or worse) from the breach. Thousands of consumers would stop doing business with the bank. The breach would make front-page headlines in the coming week. The CEO would address the issue and try to earn back consumer confidence with an expensive public relations campaign. He would last only another quarter before being asked to step down by the company's stakeholders.

Cybersecurity Is a Human Business

You've likely seen these types of cybersecurity scenarios play out 100 times over the past few years. If you are already working in the industry, you may have experienced one of these events firsthand—at least on a small scale. Cybersecurity is a field that is hyper-focused on software, assessments, technology stacks, and more (and rightfully so). It is a profession that requires hard skills to be honed and polished and practiced. But it also demands a clear understanding of what *truly* matters —of why cybersecurity actually exists as a profession.

It is important for us to begin by asking you to consider how many lives in our example were harmed by the breach scenario we just described to open this chapter. Seriously, we would like you to take a moment and try to count them. Begin with the names that were mentioned in the story and then go a step further to consider how many people's income, retirement savings, identity, or careers may have been collateral damage from that lone breach at that midsize bank. Try to imagine the impact of this one cyberattack on someone's brother or sister, parents, or aunt and uncle. Think about the inner-city schoolteacher, the firefighter, the nurse, the single mom who work two jobs. These people all have their own stories, and their daily lives and futures could have been affected by an event like this. Take a moment and imagine how it could affect the people in your own life—your parents, kids, friends, and more. You see, in cybersecurity, one moment in the quiet of a cubicle behind a keyboard and screen can impact thousands of lives "downstream" in this type of cybercrime event.

This realization should be the starting place for everyone who chooses a career in cybersecurity. From job security to financial security to consumer trust, it is always real people who are affected by the successes or failures of our work. Maybe the interesting tech and exciting innovation is what got you into this business—but you can't for too long pretend that this business is all about technology. It is undeniable that cybersecurity is ultimately a *human* business.

Cybersecurity is a field that attracts smart and highly motivated professionals, but it's no secret that it also often draws a high percentage of folks who can be more adept at dealing with programs, coding, and technical matters than dealing with people. It is also understandable that as technology and artificial intelligence quickly advance, some in this field can almost be dismissive of the real human beings affected by our work. We monitor network traffic, investigate cyberattacks, conduct penetration tests, install patches, or handle incidents, but we aren't always sitting alongside another living, breathing person in our day-to-day duties.

This is exactly why it is so important to begin with the core truth that there are real flesh and blood human beings behind every screen, keyboard, IP address, workstation, or account number and that these people are ultimately the reason our jobs exist.

Therefore, the value and dignity of humanity is the foundation on which the Cybersecurity Code of Honor is built.

In fact, we could argue that your understanding of the indisputable humanness of the cybersecurity profession is *essential* to your success both as a leader and as a practitioner. It is also true that the better you understand this, the higher your ceiling will be professionally.

Humans Have Inherent Value

Now, we don't want to jump too far into a university-style humanities lesson here, but in the entire breadth of human learning, ethic after ethic is founded on this same view about human value. From a historical perspective, as we talk about cybersecurity, it may be helpful to remember that while we are living in extraordinary technological times; this is just the *latest* technology revolution in a long line of "world technology revolutions." As different as it may feel from the rest of human history, the reality is that we have been dealing with ethical questions about our humanity through thousands of years of continuous technological change and challenges. Let's run down a few things that may help remind us why we value each other.

It is widely accepted that humans (and humans alone) have the capacity for complex and abstract reasoning and are also alone in having a "built-in" conscience. As we currently and scientifically understand the world, no other living creature possesses these qualities.

The belief in the inherent value of every human being goes back thousands of years and is generally accepted in all civilized nations. The concept of "human dignity" is the belief that all people have intrinsic value tied solely to the fact that they are human. This worth has nothing to do with class, race, gender, religion, abilities, or *any* other factor, other than being human. From ancient religious traditions that human beings are created in the image of God to the origins of Western civilization, the foundations of our culture are built on the idea that humans possess inherent value and are worthy of dignity.

Many of the best aspects of our society were derived from the idea that every person has worth and value —which is a beautiful thing when it works. Take a moment to reflect on the truth that the human beings we serve, protect, work alongside, and live with are the reasons we even follow codes of honor. *This entire book is based on the concept that all human beings have inherent value and dignity.* In our view, if you cannot accept this basic premise, we have a hard time discerning how you might be capable of executing your duties with ethical integrity.

Humans Over Technology

If we are to be successful in cybersecurity, we must recognize the simple guiding truth about the inherent humanness of our work and build our ethical framework from this foundation. This brings us to another important foundational understanding: humans are more important than technology. As cyber professionals, we serve human beings; we do *not* serve technology. Let's take a moment to remind ourselves no matter how advanced we become with the latest AI developments, whether generative AI or otherwise, it requires real flesh and blood human beings to *create* technology. We also note that technology does not create humans. Regardless of how many times you've watched *The Matrix* and *Bladerunner* or how close our real lives get to an *iRobot, Black Mirror,* or *Short Circuit* reality (or whatever next year's science fiction may portray), technology is subservient to humanity.

In our travels through tech and security conferences and seminars, we both have met people in the field that may argue differently. To be frank, this book (and the code of honor) may not be for those people who have lost perspective and bought into a narrative of technology over people. For us, and for those who will sign the code of honor, technology retains its place as a tool to serve humanity.

Given the new developments we see in tech, AI, and robotics, it's worth a look back at author Isaac Asimov's insights regarding robots. Writing in 1942, Asimov introduced his famous "Three Laws of Robotics," which focused on the *value of human beings* and on *keeping the role of technology in its proper place.* Asimov's laws are worth reviewing for the purposes of our discussion:

The First Law: A robot may not injure a human being or, through inaction, allow a human being to come to harm.

The Second Law: A robot must obey the orders given it by human beings except where such orders would conflict with the First Law.

The Third Law: A robot must protect its own existence *if such protection does not conflict with the First or Second Law.*

These point to tech's role in *serving* humanity.[5] This isn't really a controversial idea when we recognize that humanity is the creator and catalyst for technology and innovation. In some circles, the distinction between humans and technology is blurred. For our part, this growing blurriness is unhelpful and will create undue confusion. This is particularly true as we enable technology to take on certain human characteristics and functions through generative AI and machine learning. At the end of the day, let's not lose focus on the foundational truth that no matter how advanced it becomes, technology is a tool to be used by humans and can (and should) enable human flourishing.

By itself, technology has no inherent value. When we create something, its value (or lack of value) is assigned by the humans who use it. Consider the data breach story at the beginning of the chapter and the characters we introduced, from Brady and Elizabeth to Kit and Genevieve. Just for a moment, remove all the humans from that breach scenario. There are no cybersecurity professionals to be panicked, no stakeholders to suffer impact, no media to report the news, and no customers devastated by stolen identities and financial loss. If you remove the humans from the breach story, it becomes irrelevant. Without the people, the breach isn't a story at all. Whether or not you have ever articulated it, your commitment to honoring the dignity and value of real, living, breathing people provides an opportunity to work in cybersecurity.

The Solution to the Problem of Cybersecurity Is Principally a Human Solution

The quality of the people you employ or work with matters. Think about any do-it-yourself project where you have gathered all the right tools. Regardless of the tools, you can still experience an epic fail because in the end, it is not enough to have the right tools —you have to have the right people using them.

It is the *people* who make all the difference.

Whether you are in leadership or work collaboratively on a team, you know it is about the right people just as much as it is about the right tools. We know from years of experience that technology itself cannot fully solve the problems of cybersecurity. Even if you have only cursory experience in the tech field, you likely understand the current situation. While the tools we use to secure our environments get smarter, so do the tools that attackers throw at us. We are in a full-blown cybersecurity arms race, now including AI on both offense and defense, yet it is the human operators and "tool builders" who will win or lose the day.

Through the pages of this book, we will argue that the problem of cybersecurity is not principally a technical problem; it is principally a *human* problem. Therefore, the solution to cybersecurity problems is more about people than technology. While technology can help implement ethical guardrails to foster cybersecurity, fundamentally, human decision-making is vital to crafting and utilizing those guardrails. No matter how clever we make those ethical guardrails, humans will be even more clever in subverting them. Humans with a solid ethical framework and a grounding in character must direct the technology, not vice versa. It is *you* who makes the difference! It is *your* decision-making, *your* analytical skills, *your* faithful follow-ups, *your* integrity, and *your* character that are the constant differentiating factors in what we do.

Character Costs and Character Pays

It is the honor and reliability that people bring to their work each day that is every bit as important as their skill set. As cybersecurity professionals, you sit behind the wheel of a proverbial muscle car each day. To quote the famous line from Spider-Man: "With great power comes great responsibility." This is why both the medical and legal fields have governing oaths and codes of honor, because they recognize the responsibility carried in their jobs. In cybersecurity, you have an enormous amount of power. And if you don't already, you will hold keys to sensitive information, you will be able to unlock doors that no other employees can unlock, and often, the very well-being of your customers and co-workers will be in your hands. You will be counted on to be faithful to this charge.

For those of you in a leadership and hiring role, you probably already understand that it is easy to assume your people have character and integrity, so that you may empha-size technical skills and proficiencies in hiring decisions. As you consider professional development for your team, we encourage the further development of both technical and ethical decision-making skills. Without ethics and character in your people, they will make bad decisions with major consequences for your organization. Unethical employees will cost you dearly. It's not a matter of "if" but "when."

For the practitioners who are reading this right now, it is just as important to *practice* and exercise your character and decision-making muscles as it is to be attentive to build-ing your technical skills. You and your teams should actively stay on top of the latest trends and ethical dilemmas you might face. Have a plan in place for how you will act in those high-pressure situations. While we may be stating the obvious, this plan should be practiced regularly, which will allow for further development as everyone grows together and matures in their decision-making. We often hear people recommend that cybersecurity professionals spend two or more hours a week at the keyboard building new technical skills because tech is always changing. We must exercise our skills to stay fresh and up-to-date. Similarly, we would argue for spending some time, perhaps an hour every couple of weeks, on role-playing and studying real-life scenarios, so you and your team can build ethical decision-making mus-cles, which can quicken your response time and improve your decision-making during critical situations.

Whether you are a longtime cybersecurity professional or a new practitioner, having an ethical framework and prac-ticing how to apply it will pay great dividends. No matter how far removed from real people you may sit in your day-to-day cybersecurity operations, you cannot lose sight of the fact that this is a human business above all else. When we make decisions based on what is best for human beings, we are making better cybersecurity decisions.

Code-Critical Application

Read the following case study and answer the questions applying what you have learned in this chapter.

Case Study: When Security Is on the Chopping Block

Joe, the CIO of a large national healthcare technology company, has just learned that because of a forecasted recession, his division is being asked to cut its budget to maintain financial viability. The higher-ups are pointing toward cybersecurity as the cost center in his division that can most easily be downsized. The problem is that the company is also rolling out a new and innovative consumer application in a month. They cannot afford to lose developers, but can they really afford to cut the security staff and budget necessary to secure the new consumer application and the vital data it holds?

The reality is that cybersecurity staff positions and resources are on the chopping block unless a strong case is made that cuts can be found elsewhere. Joe gathers his leadership team together for a meeting—including the CISO, Gina, and the deputy CISO, Ramesh—to discuss the ramifications of the reduced budget and how best to move forward. They need to assess the impact of security cuts and decide if it is necessary to push back against the executive's directive. As they build their presentation, they must decide if they can simply affirm their superiors' suggested cutbacks and keep security "good enough" to avoid a catastrophic situation. And, of course, the questions come fast and furious about who will be hit by these budget decisions.

Gina will attempt to drill down on the budget to see what can be cut and still credibly secure the company's interests in the new product rollout. They will review key positions and security requirements as she prepares to present to the C-suite leaders. But as Joe, Gina, and Ramesh begin to look at the challenges they face with the proposed cutbacks, they begin to wonder if they shouldn't find a way to argue against cutting the security team at all.

As they brainstorm, Ramesh points out that coming out of the COVID-19 pandemic, they learned how quickly bad actors adapted to pandemic-related trends in their attack campaigns —including major increases of attacks from overseas against organizations gathering healthcare data and performing research, as well as all the phishing and related scams associated with treatments. And now, they must also consider how their new consumer application, which gathers significant amounts of healthcare data, could be affected. Gina is in favor of countering the proposed cuts by suggesting that they renegotiate contracts for licenses and existing software, which could save some money. It's a bold move, but she is also trying to protect her cybersecurity team because of the difficulty in hiring highly skilled, trustworthy people in a cybersecurity industry that faces a huge shortage of professionals with hands-on skills.

They examine the cost of breaches and ransomware incidents that other companies have experienced, especially in the healthcare space. And they study the potential cost of breaches related to the new consumer applications. Joe, eager to be responsive to the executive team's request for cuts to the security team, asks Gina to assess the cost of cutting staff positions and outsourcing that work to a managed security service provider, which could allow them to save 35% of total costs versus doing those tasks in-house. Ramesh asks the question they are all considering: will an MSSP do its job? They know from experience that sometimes they don't, letting major attacks slip through.

Ramesh also asks his boss to consider what representations the organization has made to the public about cybersecurity in advertisements and other public statements related to the new application or regarding their overall business practices. If they are going to cut the security staff or budget, should the company also make sure to remove all security representations from its marketing and ads as they could invite regulatory scrutiny and lawsuits? And, if the organization removes those assurances from its literature, will customers notice and still trust them and their brand-new product? Or, if there is a breach, and a history of those representations in the past, will the company still be held liable by regulators and the legal system?

Joe learns in a teleconference call later that day that the CEO's clear approach to the application rollout (in the face of a coming recession) is to unequivocally move forward with security team cuts and worry about security later. The company's investors have been promised that this product rollout will lead to clear growth in the next fiscal year. He believes that they can come back and take care of security after the product release and once they are certain it will be adopted by consumers. He believes they can do this without incurring harm to the company or consumers.

Of course, his approach is common in technology— Microsoft Windows didn't have a working security model for decades until Windows NT in 1993, and even NT almost shipped without the basics of file system security due to market pressure. Similarly, the Internet Protocol didn't have built-in security for decades until IPSec was formulated. Early Wi-Fi implementations lacked any sort of strong security. More recently, many Internet of Things (IoT) devices had woeful security until after they proved to be successful in the marketplace, after which security was grafted into the next generation of devices. In this vein, the CEO argues that security is often retrofitted into applications after they prove to be successful. He seems to be willing to take the risk and put out a minimum viable product, at least from a cybersecurity perspective, for their healthcare customers. Joe and his team are resigned to the reality that there is no such thing as 100% security anyway. They decide they have no choice but to move forward with the security cuts as requested by the executive team.

Critical Application Questions

The reality is that cybersecurity is always a cost center and is also usually one of the first in line to face budget cuts when economic hardships arise. Discuss how Joe and his team handled this situation. What could be done differently? What did they fail to consider?

List the number of people who could be affected by this common scenario beyond the three characters in this story. What are their roles? How could they be impacted?

How does their final decision hold up, considering what we have discussed about the value and dignity of people?

Explain your obligation to protect the people involved in a scenario like this (that can take place at any company). What is your duty to the investors, employees, customers, and other stakeholders?

While the CEO's assertion that they should roll out the application first and worry about security later may make financial sense, discuss scenarios that the company could face considering this decision.

3

To Serve and Protect

"I will seek the best interests of others."

– The Cybersecurity Code of Honor

"There is no greater calling than to serve your fellow men. There is no greater contribution than to help the weak. There is no greater satisfaction than to have done it well."

– Walter Reuther

"Love cannot remain by itself—it has no meaning. Love has to be put into action, and that action is service."

– Mother Teresa

We recently had the opportunity to watch a sharp senior security officer of a large medical firm present and field questions at a National Security Agency (NSA) cybersecurity conference about all that her organization learned from a recent attack they suffered. The audience was primarily made up of C-suite leaders who work on the periphery of our industry. She was addressing the rise in ransomware attacks and documenting the ins-and-outs of some of the more high-profile cases. She referenced some interesting details about the 2021 attack on the Colonial Pipeline, which threatened to disrupt the national petroleum distribution infrastructure, and explained how that company gave in to demands and paid the ransom.[i] Because gasoline shortages directly impact most Americans, this attack hit close to home for many consumers and was a prominently covered case of skyrocketing ransomware into public consciousness. She covered another attack in 2021 when the same notorious ransomware group that hit the Colonial Pipeline targeted a chemical distribution company. After stealing 150 GB worth of data, the attackers demanded the equivalent of $7.5 million in Bitcoin. The chemical distribution company paid $4.4 million, which at that time was the highest documented ransomware payment in history.

She also discussed how the computer giant Acer, a Taiwanese electronics and computer maker, was hit by a ransomware attack where the threat actors demanded an astonishing $50 million to restore its production facilities. The presenter explained to the audience that many of these crimes go undocumented because companies will choose to pay the ransom in silence in the hopes of making it

---

[i] Interestingly, law enforcement officers in the US were able to recover some of that money through careful sleuthing using blockchain analysis and other investigative efforts.

all go away. As you may have experienced in your own job, these types of ransomware attacks can have a devastating impact. As she continued to speak, we could feel the tension rise in the room as the chief information officers (CIOs), C-suite leaders, and those who rely on our services in the security world began to shift uncomfortably in their chairs. It was as if the entire room was communally thinking of the damage one unexpected attack could pose to their own organizations and collectively reconsidering the funding of their security teams and systems.

We Need You on That Wall

The security officer paused in that moment of her presentation on the importance of stopping these ransomware attacks and said something that struck home to everyone in the room. It was a statement of duty. It was a bold proclamation of her commitment to service. She explained matter-of-factly, "You need to know that in my position as a senior security officer, I'm awake in the middle of the night so that you don't have to be." Her affirmation was not delivered with pride or bluster. It was simply the truth. We believe her pronouncement was as clear an example of the kind of commitment reflected in the best of our cybersecurity profession as you will hear—service to our fellow human beings in helping to keep them secure is what our jobs are really all about.

Perhaps you've seen the 1992 movie *A Few Good Men* with Tom Cruise, Demi Moore, and Jack Nicholson. Or maybe you've watched clips on YouTube of the famous scene where Nicholson, an embattled commander on the witness stand, seethes back at Tom Cruise with all the passion and indignity he can muster: "You want me on that wall. You *need* me on that wall!" In many ways, this is the battle cry of those who work in our profession. Cybersecurity professionals choose to stand on that wall of protection. The reality in a world where cybercrime is estimated to be a $6 trillion[6] problem annually is that when you choose to work in cybersecurity, you are truly embracing a higher calling to serve and protect organizations and users. The sheer size and scope of the problems and challenges we face in the industry demand our very best.

No matter how much we love any aspect of cyber work, the true purpose of our job is to serve the interests of others. This greater good is our true north, our "why."

When young people join the military, they are asked to swear a vow of *service*. Even if you have never been part of the armed forces, it is probably familiar to you on some level: "I, _____, do solemnly swear (or affirm) that I will support and defend the Constitution of the United States against all enemies, foreign and domestic; that I will bear true faith and allegiance to the same. . . ." Oaths of service have long been taken by those who are committed to protecting the vulnerable.

We know from research that commitment to service is also the biggest connection to meaning and purpose in our work. But one does come before the other—the steps to service come first, and the meaning and purpose follow. Of course, we will continue to sound the alarm about the threats that lie beyond that proverbial wall constantly testing and scheming to disrupt the lives of normal people with their phishing, ransomware, exploits, and any number of new offensive inventions. But our commitment to service begins with recognizing that we indeed stand guard on a wall of protection that sustains functioning culture, vital resources, our economy, and our governments. And as technology advances, we in this industry are becoming a fundamental asset to our civilization. Yes, *you* as a cybersecurity professional are a vital part of what is needed by society. To ignore your call to service is to dismiss how vital cybersecurity is to our survival. Service begins with acknowledging that we truly need you on that wall.

Know Your Why—Purpose and People

We began by recognizing the inherent value and dignity of human beings. Now, we're focused on serving the best interests of those in your sphere of influence. That can be challenging if we do not clearly understand your *why*. So, let's consider the "why."

Research is clear that most people don't derive meaning and value of their work from salary. Money doesn't truly provide purpose. Good compensation is important, but money isn't a trustworthy sustainable motivator in any job for the vast majority of people. In numerous surveys, Millennials and people in Generation Z especially seek jobs with purpose and positive impact on society. Thankfully, cybersecurity jobs have that baked right in, as we work together in this industry to make the world a safer, more secure place.

What about the novelty and fascination of cyber work? For many people (including your two authors), it really matters that we find our job interesting. We need to be challenged intellectually and to feel engaged in the obstacles that we face day-in and day-out. New projects are motivating and provide energy. The cybersecurity field is full of interesting, challenging, and fun technical work. But we also know that novelty and challenge don't really provide lasting meaning for most people, especially over the longer term. Yes, you will have times when your work is interesting, but you also may get bored or even burned out doing the same task every day as an analyst or a penetration tester. You will have seasons of feeling challenged and engaged, and then the novelty will wear off, and you will long for advancement or to try different tasks in your daily work. Novelty and challenge aren't consistent stimuli.

So, what truly motivates us in our work? Social science research and data tell us that people are driven first and foremost by the *meaning* they find in their jobs. In other words, *why* you work matters more than what you currently find interesting, and it also matters more than your compensation. David Ulrich, an author and professor of business at the University of Michigan focused on researching management and leadership, explains, "An abundant organization enables its employees to be completely fulfilled by finding meaning and purpose from their work experience. This meaning enables employees to have personal hope for the future and create value for customers and investors."[7]

So, embracing the challenge to stand on that wall really does affect how we feel about our jobs.

The second biggest *why* in the workspace points back to what we discussed in the previous chapter, namely, the people. The opportunity to work with and for good people is an essential part of your why. As a recent article from the *Harvard Business Journal* points out, "...social connections play a central role in fostering a sense of purpose and well-being in the workplace."[8]

If you lean into your *why*—the purpose and the people—it will help you bring a servant mindset to your job. If you embrace service, studies reflect it will be beneficial for your career as well as make the world a better place. Throughout our careers, we have been fortunate to witness this impact and experience it ourselves directly, and we are deeply humbled and grateful for it.

We can't think of a better example of someone who understood his *why* more than Dan Kaminsky, an incredible security researcher who did pioneering work in tool development, vulnerability discovery, and much more, from the early 2000s up to the 2020s. Dan was dedicated to service. Of course, he was a renowned expert in the cybersecurity field, but one of the greatest reflections of his commitment to the greater good was the story of how he discovered a massive Internet vulnerability and worked tirelessly in service to the community to ensure it was handled properly.

In 2008, Kaminsky discovered a fundamental design flaw that allowed for arbitrary DNS cache poisoning, which affected nearly every DNS server on the planet. The exploit allowed attackers to impersonate any legitimate website and steal data. You might think you were accessing your bank, credit card company, or social media site, but, by exploiting the flaw Dan discovered, an attacker could redirect you to an imposter site that could seriously harm you. It took him two days to figure out that this worked on almost every nameserver in the world—a massive flaw. Dan understood that if the knowledge came out publicly, it could bring down the entire Internet or allow sneaky attackers to commit untold thefts and mayhem. So, he kept it under wraps and worked diligently and tirelessly behind the scenes to fix it. He called an emergency summit at Microsoft's headquarters to address the widespread problem. He also worked to quickly assemble a coalition that would create a fix for the vulnerability before it was disclosed to the public.

Dan was a truly incredible champion who desperately worked to make cyberspace safe and secure for the average user. Beyond his great work in helping secure DNS, Dan was constantly challenging the information security world to do better. Dan shared his truly remarkable insights and the joy of life via countless presentations at various cybersecurity conferences, via his blog, in social media, and through the cybersecurity tools he released. Sadly, Dan suddenly passed away from complications with diabetes in 2021. Dan was a hero not because of his expertise but because of his deep commitment to focusing on what was best for others—his inspirational services to the community. He continued to speak the truth about vulnerabilities (even with DNS) all the way up to his early passing, not because it was financially beneficial for him but because he was committed to a better world.

People like Dan make a difference not just because of their brilliance and talent but because they are committed to serving. You, too, can make a real impact if you embrace this ethic. This type of commitment to service happens when we keep our *why* at the center of our daily actions. Our choices as practitioners or leaders should reflect our greater purpose. That means we need to ask ourselves these simple questions each day:

Will this action serve and protect others?

Does what I am about to do truly reflect my *why*?

Think about the daily practitioner, the analyst who comes into the security operations center (SOC) and spends all day looking at alerts. Or, think about the penetration tester who hammers target systems day after day, looking for potential vulnerabilities but almost always finding nothing. Yes, this type of work can become mind-numbing or boring at times, but that analyst or penetration tester is standing watch on the wall. These people are on the digital front lines, and there will be days when the job feels tedious. One of your authors (Ed) has frequently said that some cybersecurity jobs sometimes feel like day-after-day monotonous tedium, periodically interrupted by moments of sheer exhilaration, extreme terror, or both all mixed together.

This is when you need to embrace your *why* to carry you through those periods of tedium and even terror. There will be moments when you are running late for your evening dinner reservations and stay late to brief the incoming team on an anomaly. In leadership roles, you will face tough personnel decisions—but you will meet them head-on. Your *why* is always going to require you to make sacrifices for the greater good. But each time you take a step in that direction, you will find greater purpose and meaning in your work.

Service Means Sharing: Sharing Starts with Good Communication

Putting others first and learning to practice servant leadership means sharing, and sharing is about good communication. Let's begin with a focus on communication skills. We've both been in this field for a long time, and we don't believe it is the least bit controversial to address the reality that there are communication challenges within the field of technology generally and cybersecurity in particular. That said, communication is not simply the ability to pass along information. Good communication is closely tied to the concept of emotional intelligence, often referred to as EQ.

Like other forms of intelligence, EQ isn't evenly distributed. Some people in cybersecurity have it in abundance, while some do not. Even if you don't have a strong natural EQ, you undoubtedly bring a lot of other intelligence types to the table that make you extraordinary.

EQ is the ability to understand, use, and manage your own emotions in positive ways to communicate effectively, empathize with others' emotions, overcome challenges, and defuse conflicts. It includes the ability to understand others' emotional states and tread carefully in dealing with them. In short, it is the ability to relate well to others.

While we don't want to lean too far into generalizations, we realize that cybersecurity is populated with many folks who possess very high IQs and some folks with lesser EQs. If you are in C-suite leadership on the periphery of cybersecurity, this is important to recognize, even (and perhaps especially) in yourself. Interpersonal communication skills are just a small part of the total EQ skill equation. Whether you are a young practitioner or have been in this line of work for many years, studies show that there is a direct correlation between your interpersonal skills and your career advancement. For those who may feel a little challenged on the communication front (or maybe you lead people who do), here's something we want you to understand: effective communication and even EQ are skills that can be developed and heightened through care, effort, and practice.

Like writing code several hours a week to stay sharp, communication skills and EQ can be practiced and improved. They are muscles that can be built through regular exercise. No matter how well you believe you relate to others, there are many great resources that can help you sharpen your communication skills and connect to the people around you. You can always get better. Embrace practices that improve your listening skills, self-awareness, and the ability to recognize the feelings of others.[9] Of course, the greater point is that to serve the people we work for *effectively*, the people we protect, the people we work alongside, we must learn how to interact and communicate with them effectively.

It is vital for us to communicate our expertise and experience with others. You may remain quiet due to imposter syndrome. You may be tempted to think maybe you shouldn't speak up because you just aren't sure. The old expression to "be silent as to not be thought a fool" can be a powerful motivator. While there are times to heed that idea, it can also impede a lot of important and much-needed interaction. We need each other in this line of work, and we need to foster a work environment with open communication and collaboration. If you are in leadership, make sure you are providing a safe space for your team to share what they have learned with each other and to push back on policies and/or practices that threaten your cybersecurity. During team meetings, explicitly seek input from *everyone* on the team, and reach out and kindly encourage everyone on your team to contribute their thoughts and insights. Great communication can patch holes in the wall by helping us lean into each other's strengths.

Sharing with the Broader Cyber Community: We Are All on the Same Wall

Being committed to serve and protect goes beyond our obligation to our organization, as the story of Dan Kaminsky reflects. Our ethical decision-making for those in our sphere of influence in turn also influences the greater good. We commend leaders and practitioners to set competition and rivalry aside and to consider the security of our cybersecurity community at large. It means embracing the idea that we are all part of that wall of defense.

We compete in business, because we want our organizations to succeed, and we want career success. But we should not compete in cybersecurity. We encourage you to share your knowledge and expertise with colleagues who are on the same side. This means sharing threat intelligence and proven defensive strategies with competitors in your industry— yes, even when market share or revenue is on the line.

This type of commitment is illustrated by what happened with Target and Walmart.

In 2005 and 2006, Walmart was the victim of a serious security breach when cybercriminals targeted the chain's point-of-sale system and siphoned sensitive data to a computer in Eastern Europe. Years later, Walmart competitor Target was hacked through a heating and air conditioning subcontractor that had worked at several locations at the retailer. The breach had compromised data with the names, mailing addresses, phone numbers, email addresses, and payment card information for up to 70 million people.

These competitive retailers now actively share threat intelligence with each other and with the U.S. government through the Retail and Hospitality Information Sharing and Analysis Center (RH-ISAC). The collaboration of retailers and related industries has enabled analysts to be on the lookout for real-time cyber threats such as new strains of malware, activity on underground forums, and potential software vulnerabilities. Data-sharing initiatives that used to be rare now seem like a commonsense move.[10] We are seeing communication and cooperation between these two industry competitors and more of the attitude that Tony Sager, a senior vice president and chief evangelist for the Center for Internet Security (CIS), promotes: "Let my getting hacked help you improve your defenses. Let my compromise improve your detection." He is right, of course, because of our *why*. After all, we are all ultimately defending the same wall.

Checking In

We are responsible for serving the interests of others in our work. It is part of our *why*. Practically speaking, what does it look like to serve and protect others in your daily work? Think about it and make some notes. We suggest the following checklist to help you more deeply consider your *why* and answer whether you are putting service first in your work:

- Serving the best interests of others means your employer, customers, and stakeholders.

    In your job role, who are you defending and how? Make a list.

    Who are you keeping more secure?

    How are you serving them?

    What are some practical ways you can focus on service?

- Defending the vulnerable is our duty, which is quickly becoming a bigger population.

    How does your position enable you to do this?

    How can you be better equipped to defend the vulnerable?

    Do you put the greater good ahead of financial gain, competition, and career advancement? How so?

    Do you have any examples of where you have done so in the past?

    How can you change to focus more on that?

- Making cyber defenders stronger should be of great interest. It is your obligation to seek to share your experience and knowledge with others in your workplace and the community more generally. How do you make the people around you better?

A Final Example

One of our favorite examples of servant leadership is an icon in cybersecurity. He is a great example of how approaching work with a service mindset can spread through your entire life. You may be familiar with Chris Sanders, the notable cybersecurity author, analyst, and instructor. Chris is on the front lines of innovation and training in cybersecurity. But, in addition to all his great work contributions, Chris also founded and directs the Rural Technology Fund (RTF), which is a nonprofit organization focused on providing science, technology, engineering, and mathematics (STEM) education opportunities for children in rural areas.

Growing up in Kentucky, Chris witnessed firsthand how high-paying tech jobs can help end generational poverty in rural families and lift entire communities. He started the RTF in 2008 to help introduce rural students to the potential of technology careers and equip them with the education they needed to pursue those jobs. Of course, rural students often have fewer opportunities for exposure to technology than their urban or suburban counterparts, greatly limiting their ability to pursue tech-related careers. His organization strives to give students the opportunity to explore cutting-edge career paths, bring technology to life, and imagine their future as one with limitless creative potential. Chris isn't just serving on the wall of defense in the cybersecurity field—his service extends to touch the lives of thousands of students in his community. We hope you will see the value in following his lead and find your own ways to embrace service. We challenge you to think like a servant in all areas of your life.

Code-Critical Application

Read the following case study and answer the questions applying what you have learned in this chapter.

Case Study: Responsible Disclosure of a Security Flaw

Karen and Luke are security researchers working for a company that creates a cyber defense product. Their main duties are to investigate mobile apps, determine their flaws, and try to develop appropriate security responses integrated in their product. Of course, their company benefits when researchers like Karen and Luke discover vulnerabilities that get people's attention. Yesterday, they discovered a huge flaw and are meeting with their supervisor, Ben, to decide whether they should release that information publicly. Ben is already dead set on releasing the information and really isn't interested in objections. Even so, they spend the first half of the meeting presenting the pros and cons of a quick release. Ben asserts his belief that once they go public with the information, it will drive the vendor to develop and release a patch more quickly. Luke adds that it may also push the public and defenders to apply that fix more quickly to block exploitation by potential attackers.

The flaw they have discovered happens to be part of an increasingly popular social networking app gaining thousands of new users every day. Ben is convinced that the notoriety gained by exposing the information would bring them some great press and would also be advantageous for the firm's revenue. Karen objects because she believes if the vulnerability is released too quickly, it could lead to criminals leveraging the flaw to harm the public before a fix is available. The three also consider the dark reality that unscrupulous governments could use the flaw to exploit journalists, dissidents, and others.

Still, they wrestle with how the scenario will unfold and affect the public. Will the vendor or company even feel the need to fix the flaw? If they don't, are they sure that it would result in a malicious actor exploiting it? Is there a timeframe in which they can responsibly disclose the flaw to still ensure the vulnerability gets fixed without jeopardizing the safety and security of the public and community? Ben ultimately decides to ignore the suggestions of his team members and moves forward with releasing the information to the public without notifying the social networking company in advance so public users can be alerted to the risks in using the program. He feels it is also the best course of action for their firm.

Critical Application Questions

What challenges does this type of discovery present from the standpoint of serving and protecting the greater community? Who do you believe is right in this scenario?

How do you feel about Ben's response to the concerns of his team members? Does it reflect the kind of "EQ" that you would expect from leadership? How could he have handled the situation differently?

In this scenario, what would you do if the social media platform chose not to fix the problems you had discovered if you notified them in advance?

How can you apply what you have learned about putting others first to this common cybersecurity scenario? Discuss any similar experiences you have had and how you or your team handled those cases.

4

"Zero-Day" Humanity and Accountability

"I will strive to recognize, take ownership, and appropriately communicate my mistakes and exercise patience toward others who make errors."

— The Cybersecurity Code of Honor

"Mistakes are a fact of life. It is the response to error that counts."

— Nikki Giovanni

"It is unwise to be too sure of one's own wisdom. It is healthy to be reminded that the strongest might weaken and the wisest might err."

— Mahatma Gandhi

Matt is a security engineer for one of the world's most widely used fintech platforms. He has been with the company for nearly four years and quickly worked his way up through the ranks from analyst to engineer because of his coding background and coding proficiency. He is driven and bright and is currently up for another promotion, specifically because of a new security program that his team designed and implemented last quarter. Days ago, Rima, a newer member of Matt's design team, discovered what she believed was a flaw in their new program. The flaw seemed to be the result of simple errors the team made in the development process. When she presented it to Matt, he quickly decided it wasn't significant enough to raise any alarms. He dismissed it as a minor defect that likely wouldn't be exploited and could be addressed sometime down the road. After all, his team had already been recognized at last week's company meeting for their innovation, and program implementation was already full steam ahead.

Bad Decisions and Multiplication

But as the week unfolds, it becomes clear that the flaw Matt chose to overlook has already been discovered and exploited. News hasn't spread through the research community as far they can tell right now—so far, the team only has evidence of a few small examples of sample data being pilfered via exploitation of the flaw. Rima urges Matt to share the problem with the appropriate supervisors, but he convinces her that it can be fixed "in-house" (among the team) *before* it becomes a larger problem. He believes there is no need to worry the executive team or the senior security officer and argues that they can't even be sure about the extent of the vulnerability. Matt's team meets to discuss the situation and to patch the problem as quickly as they can. Of course, his team doesn't understand that they are able to see only a small part of the larger issue. Because this initial compromise goes unreported up the chain of command, the rest of the company doesn't take notice as attackers continue to use this flaw as a doorway to steal information. One bad choice is about to multiply into a host of problems.

Days later, this small "departmental" fire turns into a four-alarm crisis when attackers release 30 million usernames, email addresses, and phone numbers of customers of banks that rely on the platform. The coming internal investigation will likely result in Matt being fired. But the damage is done. Customers who trusted the platform have been compromised.

This scenario involving Matt and his team could have been avoided by quickly recognizing that no one is perfect and that mistakes need to be brought to light and addressed ASAP. The biggest problem wasn't the team's technical mistakes—it was Matt's poor response to those mistakes. As a leader, he made decisions based on self-interest rather than protecting his company and its user base. But his team is also culpable.

This raises an important point. One option for Rima would have been to go directly to her chief information security officer (CISO) with her concerns. Doing so may have seen the problem quickly addressed and avoided. Perhaps so, but this course of action creates its own unique problem: going around your direct supervisor is generally not a good idea. It's a good way to get on the wrong side of your boss, and perhaps even fired.

We don't think anyone should easily or quickly go around their supervisor. As such, in a dilemma like this, we recommend you seek the counsel of an objective third party who is not directly in your line of reporting relationships, always respecting private information and nondisclosure agreements. Later in this book, we'll discuss the importance of having a good mentor who can provide wise counsel at times like this.

The mistakes in this scenario are seemingly small. They are the kind of "insignificant" choices you may find yourself making without much thought. But they are *exactly* the type of decisions that can snowball into a crisis in cybersecurity.

Matt's story reflects why accountability and professional transparency are so essential. It also highlights the fact that no one is perfect. Humans make mistakes. And beyond simple, innocent mistakes, we sometimes make decisions based on self-interest, ignoring others' needs and interests. We can lose sight of the true north and make compromised decisions. No one is immune. *No one*. We work in a human business, and that means we all deal with the realities of being human.

Humans Are Flawed

No matter how flawless we may think we can be in our day-to-day work, we all have a built-in "zero-day" vulnerability. For those on the periphery of cybersecurity, a *zero-day* vulnerability is the discovery of a previously unknown flaw for which there is no currently available fix in a system. It's pretty clear that every human being has a similar inherent flaw built into our DNA. The inherent imperfection of every human being is a cornerstone of our ethical conversation. It is the very reason that we need the Cybersecurity Code of Honor to help guide our decisions and practices. This is why we need a commonly accepted set of guiding principles to apply to our actions and decisions.

No matter how brilliant, disciplined, well-run, well-led, or well-designed our team may be, no matter how many checks and balances we have in place, you can be certain that mistakes will be made. Many of the great religions of history have addressed our innate fallibility and tried to manage the consequences of human frailty and imperfection. There is no magic to inoculate us from our tendency to make mistakes or act in our self-interest. It is part of our "programming" and the nature of the imperfect and difficult world we face.

Real problems arise when we believe that we are without flaws. Anyone who has ever been married or had a long-term roommate has been confronted with their own imperfections. Denying them often creates more problems than the imperfections themselves. Anyone who has children knows that they don't need to be taught to behave badly. Parents constantly address the decisions and consequences of their children's poor choices. All of these imperfections come naturally.

Turning Vulnerability into Strength: It Begins with Humility

Fortunately, there are ways to help minimize our human "zero-day" vulnerability. By recognizing our inherent imperfection, we take a vital step toward transforming that vulnerability into a strength. *This is one of the cornerstones to building a great team and work community.*

It begins with the ancient virtue of humility. While humility is not easy or natural for most of us, it's not as daunting as you might think. It is perhaps the most important quality to help mitigate mistakes. Humility is for everyone, from the beginner all the way up to the boss. Whether you are a first-year analyst, an experienced 20-year industry guru, or an accomplished CISO, we will all be faced with the reality of sometimes making the wrong choice.

If humility is part of a work culture, it's likely because the leaders display and model humility for their teams. Jim Collins, author of the best-selling book *Good to Great*, argues that humility is one of the core traits of the finest leaders, whom he refers to as "Level 5 Leaders." He explains, "The best CEOs in our research display tremendous ambition for their company combined with the stoic will to do whatever it takes, no matter how brutal (within the bounds of the company's core values), to make the company great. Yet at the same time, they display a remarkable *humility* about themselves, ascribing much of their success to luck, discipline, and preparation rather than personal genius."

Humility unlocks a sequence of dominos. It is the basis by which we recognize our vulnerability that by being human, we are flawed and not perfect. Imperfection puts all of us on a level playing field. Once we recognize our vulnerability for making mistakes, it provides the foundation for taking ownership of them. When we take ownership of our mistakes, we are more willing to communicate them appropriately. And if we're owning and appropriately communicating our mistakes, knowing we are all flawed, we have gained the ability to handle the mistakes of others.

None of this is easy, but it is possible. And it provides for a healthy and open culture. A good way to keep a check on your ego and exercise humility involves asking yourself a series of questions when you are making a decision and are about to settle on an approach. Ask yourself:

- Why am I pursuing this approach?
- Is this all about my own benefit?
- Who else benefits from this approach? Is it just me?
- Who could potentially be hurt by this approach?
- What's best for my organization overall? What's best for my employees? What's best for my boss?
- How does this approach benefit or hurt our customers and other stakeholders?
- Are there other options that I've overlooked that might be more optimal for everyone involved?

For Matt, in the opening story, practicing humility would have meant going to leadership immediately with the possible problem rather than theoretically protecting himself from being blamed for a hole that could be exploited. He rolled the dice and lost. Unnecessarily.

There are constant examples of this kind of humility and accountability throughout the industry. In 2022, a company called Okta publicly acknowledged a mistake in handling a cyberattack by an extortion group. The company released a very candid statement explaining to the public that they simply didn't know the extent of the breach they were dealing with at the time. It is an apology that reflects humility as they explain that they should've been more forthcoming with consumers and proactive in their response to the breach.

Part of their statement read: "At that time, we didn't recognize that there was a risk to Okta and our customers. . . . Considering the evidence that we have gathered in the last week, it is clear that we would have made a different decision if we had been in possession of all of the facts that we have today."[11] Of course, it's easy to be critical of the situation or even cynical about the confessional response. But sooner or later, we will all face a similar situation, perhaps many of them. We consider this a good example of a company owning up to a mistake with appropriate transparency, especially when compared to revelations about other companies that have been exposed by former employees for covering up vulnerabilities.

Okta's admission that they mishandled the breach demonstrates how humility can turn vulnerability into strength.

They are accomplishing so much with this type of response: promoting transparency, signaling a course-correction as an organization, and setting an example for other companies. Sadly, Okta again suffered a breach in 2023. Initial reports in October 2023 were that the attackers accessed data for only 1% of Okta customers in their support system. But later investigations in November showed that all Okta customers, some 18,000 organizations, had some data exposed to attackers. Okta admitted not only the breach also but that its earlier exposure estimates were incorrect. We can learn from the mistakes of others. When we are honest about our mistakes, it is a model for others to consider, and it can open the door for better solutions.

Our friend shared a great story of his 4-year-old son's moment in an upstairs bathroom that reflects the nature of what happens when we don't own our mistakes in cybersecurity. As the toilet began to overflow, the little boy panicked. He didn't want to come downstairs to tell his parents, so instead, he closed the bathroom door, locked it from the outside, and snuck back to his room to play. Once the door was closed, everything would be perfectly fine, right? Just think about how many times we quietly "lock the door" on a problem, sneak down the hall, and hope that there won't be consequences. For many people, it's a natural instinct to pretend the problem doesn't exist and hope for the best.

Our friend and his wife explained their perspective on the event. They were enjoying preparing dinner for the family in the kitchen after a long day at work. They were so busy that they didn't notice the ceiling above them begin to change color. They didn't notice the drywall in the ceiling above them began to bulge and take on strange shapes. They still missed it when a few drops of dirty water began to drip behind them into the middle of the kitchen floor. They were listening to music, talking about their day, and laughing when one of them finally turned and stepped into what had become a large puddle on the kitchen floor. And at that very moment, murky brown water began to pour from the ceiling like a rainstorm. They ran upstairs to find the bathroom door locked, water streaming underneath the door and down the carpeted hallway. Needless to say, dinner wasn't served that evening. In fact, it would be a week of fast-food meals with the kids until they could even go near the kitchen again. Of course, it was quite expensive to repair the ceiling, the water damage to the kitchen floor, the carpet, and the plumbing. All of this could've been avoided if their son, little Eli, would've just come for help instead of trying to hide something that had gone wrong. What an apt metaphor for the importance of not hiding mistakes or vulnerabilities and instead taking ownership and seeking help.

Being a Lifelong Learner

In our roles as both businesspeople and educators, one of our greatest desires for those who are in our employ, or our students, is that they become lifelong learners. For someone to become a lifelong learner, they must recognize that there is plenty they don't know. It's the clear mindset that no one has all the answers. Because we work in higher education and cybersecurity, we're surrounded by a lot of smart people. We've encountered, and you have too, people whose intelligence sometimes gets in their own way. They are not good listeners, talk too much, and generally come across as thinking they have all the answers. No one really likes a "know-it-all." The best and most effective leaders and workers we know are people who readily admit what they don't know.

Curiosity—wondering about something new or how to fix a problem—is the driver for innovation in technology. We encourage a student outlook reflecting the famous observation of Conrad Hall, noted cinematographer and philosopher: "You are always the student, never the master. Keep moving forward." This is echoed in all areas of our field. You are always a student in technology because the rapid evolution of the industry demands that you be a student.

We are regularly reminded of the need to keep learning by our experience in hiring people. Neither of us has kept count, but we are humbled by the large number of hires we've gotten wrong. Between us, we have more than 50 years of hiring experience. You would think by now we'd get it right every time. Well, think again.

We estimate that, over the years, we've gotten about two-thirds of our hires correct—that is, the right person in the right job at the right time. That's great, except it means we've gotten about one-third wrong, sometimes with a small impact and sometimes with enormously painful implications. That's pretty humbling. The point is that we are always trying to get better at assessing and hiring staff. Learning how to make great hires is an ongoing process. Why? Because people change, employees change, work culture and expectations change, generations change, and we need to adapt and adjust our thinking to stay current with it and at the same time be faithful to our principles. Whatever role you are in, we encourage you to stay curious. Stay hungry to learn and grow.

Handling the Mistakes of Others

Recognizing our own imperfections and mistakes sets the stage for how we handle the mistakes of others. This self-awareness should help develop patience.

None of us works in a vacuum. We are surrounded by people who we depend upon. If you are in leadership, your people are going to make mistakes and come up short at times. If you are on a team, you are going to run into errors that your teammates make—just as you tend to mess up occasionally. We believe that an important part of this whole equation is extending grace and patience to others for their own zero-day vulnerabilities.

If you are in leadership, you probably have heard the "failing forward" thoughts about business. You can probably look back on your career and see that you haven't advanced because you are perfect; *you have moved forward because of your willingness to learn from your failures*. As Mary Tyler Moore, actress and film producer, once said, "Mistakes are part of the dues one pays for a full life." It is vital that we not only embrace that ethic of learning through our mistakes for ourselves but practice that in the way we judge and hold other people accountable. In leadership, we always need to acknowledge the truth as communicated by the great jazz musician Duke Ellington: "We should recognize that everybody is capable of making a mistake, and we should not raise any more hell about somebody else's mistakes than we expect to be raised when we make one."

Let's Try to Avoid "Breaking Bad"

Not only is everyone capable of making *mistakes*, but it is also important to embrace the truth that everyone is fully capable of making unethical choices. As much as we aren't perfect in the daily execution of our jobs, we are also all susceptible to making bad choices. If we are being honest, we are always just one shade away from being the kid in the grocery store who slips the pack of gum in their pocket when their parents aren't watching. If you're raising an eyebrow here, let's simply ask the following questions: When was the last time you cut corners at work? When was the last time you bent the rules for your own benefit? When was the last time you took a longer break than you were supposed to? When was the last time you moved a small "inconsequential" number on that budget just to make sure it lines up with projections? When was the last time you shaded the truth to your boss? When was the last time you hid what you thought was a small mistake?

All too often, the bad choice isn't nefarious or premeditated; we do it out of convenience. If you've never done anything questionable, we'd certainly like to meet you! At some point, we all fall into this trap one way or another.

It's human nature. We remind you of this because it is important to stay diligent by being reflective about the decisions we make and holding them up to the light of our ethical guiding principles. Why? Because even small unethical choices can lead to larger ones.

One bad decision can snowball. One lie or unethical choice can lead to another and another, and before you know it, you are "breaking bad." If you haven't seen the popular streaming series about the high school science teacher named Walter White, it is a great example of how one bad decision can lead anyone down the wrong path. In the show, Walter makes some questionable decisions to pay his medical bills when facing a debilitating terminal disease. He's understandably in a difficult place in life. He starts out as a decent enough guy. He's doing this "for his family." But those first few bad choices are compounded when he must work to cover them up, and that leads to another round of bad decisions to cover his tracks and so on. As the series goes on, Walter's decision-making spirals into great darkness, including crime, murder, and great cruelty. At some point, he reaches a point of no return—he has "broken bad." And, of course, throughout the entire series, you are occasionally reminded that Walter's criminal behavior was originally self-justified by his motive to financially provide for his family after getting a cancer diagnosis.

We aren't really being dramatic here. If you have kids, think how a direct question like "Did you eat that cookie?" can spiral off into a series of lies. Shortcuts happen. Sometimes that lie is the first thing that comes to mind. We are often tempted to be dishonest or do the wrong thing because it seems small and inconsequential. And we often confuse taking the shortcut with choosing the path of least resistance and lying. But in cybersecurity, there is a guiding and consistent truth about these mistakes: *escalation* happens fast.

Consider for a moment if you, as a cybersecurity or IT admin with great access to your computing environment, decide to look at private data associated with certain customers or other employees of your organization. Or you happen to look through timestamps just to see when they are logged in. Such seemingly innocent snooping over time becomes easier to do. Then, it escalates to reviewing that person's profile. But then suddenly, this nefarious new activity of snooping around is in the logs, and a supervisor is going to see that you did it. So, what do you do to protect yourself from your mistakes? You edit or delete the logs. But there's another logging server you don't have direct access to, yet it's got a common vulnerability, ripe for exploitation, that can give you the access you need to alter the logs. Now, what started out as simple prying out of boredom leads to hacking your own organization to cover your tracks. This is just one example of how quickly escalation can happen.

Bad decisions need not be premeditated. They can come about by opening a file here and there and, "before we know it," we are knee-deep in a different kind of reality. As in, before you know it, you are looking into a music star's surgery information and leaking it to TMZ (yes, this actually happened). You can read story after story of how these "before you know it" situations end up with the authorities knocking on your office or home door.

We all need to be accountable for our actions. None of us are truly independent agents. We may think we don't need accountability, but this is never true in the larger picture. We all live under a legal system that allows some behaviors and prohibits others. There are federal, state, and local laws that, if we break them, have consequences. Likewise, if you work for an employer, you are accountable to the rules and regulations put forth by your employer. If you don't abide by them, you risk losing your job.

It is high-risk to operate by situational ethics, meaning choosing what feels right at the moment and trying to justify things as we go along, without an ethical framework or model to guide our thinking. The practical outcome of trying to make ethical decisions by our situational feelings is that there are no guidelines to make ethical decisions. In our society, this approach is often what we have today, and it's not working very well. We believe a clear set of ethical principles is essential for good decision-making.

Since humans naturally make decisions based on self-interest, we need other people who can help guide our decision-making when things get murky. We will talk at length about the importance of mentors a little later in the book, but we believe it is vital to have folks in your life whom you can go to with questions when necessary. Mentors can be great for accountability and advice. But it is also so important to recognize that we can create good habits to help us improve and stay on top of our ethical decision-making. We can practice making good choices. And that starts by being reflective about your decisions.

How to Develop a Reflective Practice

Reflecting on your ethical choices is a habit—one you can practice each day and improve on. It is just as important as technical skill development. We believe it is beneficial to your career (and your life) to establish some routines that will allow you to be thoughtful about your decision-making.

Any reflective practice begins with intentionally setting aside time to pause and focus. We both have a habit of taking morning walks to have space and uninterrupted quiet time to think about our daily decision-making. There are too many ways to do this to list here, but we suggest that you carve out intentional moments to review your decisions from the day before and evaluate them. It is helpful to do this with what you have ahead on your calendar. Make a list of the things you know you will face in the day ahead and allow yourself to start considering and weighing those decisions and interactions.

It is extremely beneficial to think through different scenarios you may be faced with and mentally decide how to handle them. Every decision and every situation is different. How will you apply your ethical principles? How will you apply the code of honor to your decision-making? Here are some questions we consider in our own daily reflective practice:

What major decisions did I make yesterday? Do they seem appropriate now that I have had time to think them through?

Were my choices good or bad? Do I need to take ownership of a mistake? Do I need to call or apologize for something I did or did not do? Do I need to fix something or otherwise improve a situation where I didn't behave optimally upon further reflection?

What is coming up today that will require my attention? What can I learn from yesterday? How can I be better?

It is sound management to talk with your team or co-workers as you work through these critical decisions. Not every choice needs to be made by committee, but make sure you are making use of the wisdom, innovation, and expertise of the people around you. No one can be successful working as a lone wolf in this profession. Of course, following through on what you find in your daily reflective practice is vital; it is important to act if you find you made a mistake or a bad decision. Go back and tell someone who can help you correct it. And if it is something that can't be corrected, remember the truth that owning up to a bad decision is the only way to stem the escalation of further consequences. Owning up to our mistakes can be scary as a practitioner, but it is the only way to stay the course. As leaders, we need to remember to be measured and gracious when our people own their mistakes. After all, we can make that zero-day vulnerability a strength only if we learn to lean on each other.

Code-Critical Application

Read the following case study and answer the questions applying what you have learned in this chapter.

Case Study: To Pay or Not to Pay—A Ransomware Quandary

Robert in the HR department immediately called when he noticed a payment screen for ransomware pop up on his computer. He contacted Jeannie and Chris on the security team, and they quarantined the system and verified the infection. Jeannie spent the day cleaning up that machine and met with the senior security team leader, Justin, to recap the day and assess the situation. Chris, Jeannie, and Justin decide that the ransomware is not spreading on the internal network. The team, including poor Robert in HR, breathes a collective sigh of relief.

The next day, Robert receives an email from the ransomware crew claiming that they've not only encrypted sensitive data on his system but also exfiltrated it before encrypting it. They ask for $1 million in Bitcoin to be paid in the next eight hours. If their demands aren't met, they will publish all the sensitive information they exfiltrated from the organization involving the Social Security numbers of more than four million customers. In an attempt to legitimize their claims, the ransomware scammers sent an email that included the valid Social Security number of the company CISO, Jennifer: "We will publish the data we retrieved from your company. . .FYI: *YOUR CISO's* SSN is 123-45-6789." It is clear now that Jeannie, Chris, and Justin missed something in their diagnosis of the problem.

The three of them meet briefly with their CISO, Jennifer, to discuss what to do next. They are one phone call away from sharing this information with the executive team, but there are some serious concerns before pulling that big alarm. What can they find in a quick investigation, and what evidence do they have that the data was actually exfiltrated? Can they truly confirm that attackers stole the data? Jennifer points out that just because the ransomware actors have a single Social Security number (her own) doesn't necessarily guarantee there was a widespread breach. In fact, Jeannie reminds them of what they have all experienced before: it is extremely difficult to determine so early in the process whether the attackers have the data they claim to have. Furthermore, they also understand that the specific method used by the attacker to infiltrate the environment may not be identified until weeks or perhaps even months later. After discussing the issue at length, Jennifer decides that there is too much at stake not to communicate the possible breach up the chain of command.

They bring in the chief executive officer (CEO), George, to assess the situation and ascertain the most effective response. Again, the security team is transparent about the fact that they may have initially misevaluated the investigation into Robert's laptop. As his CISO sits next to him in the meeting, Justin lays out all the possible scenarios to his executive leadership—George is there along with the chief financial officer (CFO), the chief operating officer (COO), and the chief information officer (CIO). They have an entirely new set of questions to consider.

Jennifer and George point out that the first order of business is to decide if they should contact law enforcement. They must consider how that may change the case. Additionally, when is the right time to contact the insurance company? The CFO points out that if they wait too long to involve their insurance company in the discussion, they probably won't cover any losses from ransomware. The chief legal officer (CLO), meaning the general counsel, also needs to be clear on what the law requires they do—properly notifying law enforcement, regulators, the insurance company, employees, customers, the public, shareholders, and more.

Then the conversation turns to considering whether they should pay the ransom. Of course, as Justin points out, even if the organization pays, there is no guarantee that the information still won't be leaked. And, if the organization pays, it has confirmed to the criminal world that it is willing to pay a ransom, which may bring the same attacker or copycats back for more crimes.

The concern of the chief communications officer (CCO) is when or if the company should communicate its mistakes to its customers. Should they disclose this information to the public? Will it undermine consumer confidence if they do? And in addition to customers, if the CISO's information was exposed, it could mean that other employees' data may have been exposed as well. How will this impact employee morale?

George, the CEO, points out that the ransom demand does seem to be a relatively small request, given the multimillion-dollar ransoms so common in such attacks today. He asks Jennifer if that means the attackers are less sophisticated? This opens the floor to discuss the cost of paying versus not paying the ransom. The leadership team considers the implications on the organization's reputation. Maybe they would look more trustworthy to their customers and employees by paying the ransom to prevent the data from being exposed. If they don't pay, the attorney points out that there may be lawsuits from customers whose data is exposed, perhaps even a class-action suit. What are the potential costs of those lawsuits? Could regulators mount similar investigations or suits?

The executive team ultimately decides that they will not contact the authorities. They pay the ransom to protect their customers and employees. This is done in protest by their CISO, Jennifer, who doesn't believe that the attackers have the information they claim to have. The organization also launches a review of how the incident was handled by Chris and Jeannie initially and what they need to do companywide to shore up any future breaches. The focus on policy turns to what needs to be put in place proactively so that what happened through Robert's computer will not happen again. The organization builds an enterprise-wide policy and incident handling process for addressing ransomware and periodically tests this process through annual tabletop exercises (TTXs). While they weren't prepared in advance last time, they were determined not to let that happen again.

Critical Application Questions

How does the security team deal with making the mistake in assessing the initial breach? Does the leadership team handle the situation well? Why or why not?

How do you feel about the final decision to pay the ransom and keep the information in-house? How does that hold up to the ethical principles we discussed in this chapter?

Does the CISO or security professionals have an ethical responsibility to go above their leadership and share information about the breach with the authorities or other entities who could be compromised? Why or why not?

What would you do if you were in the same situation that Jennifer, the CISO, finds herself in? How would you respond to the mistake by the security team? How would you handle your superiors deciding on a response that you didn't agree with?

Have you been had a similar experience with a practitioner level or at a leadership level? Did you take time to reflect on that situation? Were you happy with your decision-making? Were there questions you faced in that scenario that weren't considered by the executive team? How would you have handled things differently?

5

It Begins and Ends with Trust

"I will be honest, trustworthy, and above reproach in my actions and communications."

– The Cybersecurity Code of Honor

"You build trust with others each time you choose integrity over image, truth over convenience, or honor over personal gain."

– John C. Maxwell, author and expert on leadership

"Being consistent in your behavior is a great way to build trust."
"People are less likely to see you as a threat if they know they can trust you."

– Germany Kent, journalist, author, and producer

Xiang had just accepted a promotion at his small liberal arts college in the Midwest. He had been with the college since graduation and had worked for years to earn the trust and respect of the college administrators to become the head of IT. He had already made headway in bolstering cybersecurity on campus after alerting the board of trustees that a neighboring state university was reporting hundreds of aggressive scans and exploitation attempts per day, all originating from a single country. But Xiang also had concerns about establishing trust and credibility with his ever-growing cybersecurity and IT team. As Xiang began to train a new security analyst, Alana, and institute new policies and procedures with the human resources department at the college, he simply used the wisdom he gained working his first high school job at a local burger joint. He remembered how his manager would ask him to come sit in her office while she counted out the cash drawers at the end of every shift while he observed to ensure all was on the up-and-up. He wanted to apply that same type of accountability to the college's security operations. He was always mindful the simple lessons of trust and accountability he had learned in his part-time job.

Weeks into Xiang's new leadership position, Alana approached him with a report about suspicious activity originating from the office of a prominent computer science professor on campus. This professor, Dr. Stevens, was a high-profile and well-published member of the academic community, who also had close ties to members of the college's board of trustees. Alana's analysis of the logs indicated that the professor seemed to be trying to access files associated with the research of some of his colleagues without permission, including personal files and even sensitive research drafts. Xiang called the head of human resources and set a time for them to meet in his office to review the logs associated with Dr. Stevens' accounts. Those activities could merit termination per university policy, but not without questions from some of the leadership. If Alana had been left on her own to handle the situation, things could have become difficult. Xiang had the right procedures in place to add to the credibility of the investigative process. But equally as important, he had built up years of trust with the college's president.

Xiang's reputation had little to do with his IT skills or vast security knowledge. The college president trusted him because he had been honest, even when it was inconvenient. He had been transparent about the failures of his IT department as well as the successes. He had been responsible with the departmental budget. He had been fair in his dealings with the staff around campus. In short, Xiang had done the investment work to build deep reservoirs of trust with his superiors. When the time came for him to present information that could lead to the termination of a prominent employee, no one questioned his motives or his presentation of the facts.

The Secret of Success

We live in a culture that cannot put down its smartphone and spends a lot of time with sensational viral videos and reactive soundbites that are generally not helpful.

One philosopher, Dallas Willard, called it a "culture flying upside down." We can become fixated on silly feats, weird skills, unique obscure talents, and over-the-top performances, but little of this contributes anything useful to our lives, let alone anything good. The growing proliferation of misinformation (both accidentally incorrect and purposely fake) contributes to the larger cultural erosion of trust that has accelerated in recent years.

Trust matters. It is one of the most important elements of a successful career and of meaningful relationships. The two are related: meaningful, trust-based relationships are essential to most successful careers. Some of the key ingredients to building trust are consistency, responsibility, and honesty. Trust is a precious quality and resource.

You may think that no one else has your red teaming skills, no one can threat-hunt quite like you, no one else is as good at forecasting the budget, or no one has led your division to this kind of growth. Any of these things may be true, but without the earned trust of those in your organization, they will likely lead you to an unstable career and perhaps much worse. In a world that celebrates fast growth and the fireworks of quick success, trust is almost an agricultural process. Trust takes seasons to build. Trust is not especially complicated; rather, it is a relatively simple, straightforward, and slow-growing quality. It is also fragile.

Think about the very first time you got behind the wheel of a car. Remember the excitement when you were handed the keys and pulled out of the driveway all by yourself. You had a tank full of gas, an open road, and perhaps a time you were expected to return. Your parents may have also been tracking your location with some app. Driving on your own required a measure of trust, and as you earned additional trust with responsible action, you likely had more incremental freedom. This trust is built step-by-step. You had to put in some practice hours. Maybe you had to take a driving class at school. You had to pass some driving tests. You had to earn the trust from your parents (or guardians) before they let you steer a ton and a half of steel, plastic, and wheels onto the street by yourself. And earning the license to drive was a slow, likely uneventful process, which is how trust is accrued.

As we illustrated in the story about Xiang, one of the keys to advancement in your career is *trust*. In cybersecurity, in addition to your technical knowledge, trust is as central as anything to success. Whether it is the boss, shareholders, your team, your co-workers, or other employees—they must be able to put those proverbial cyber keys in your hands and feel good about it. We talk about "zero-trust" architectures for our security technology infrastructures. It is a common industry phrase that reflects the "trust but verify" element that has long been part of the conversation in the world of international politics. But it also reflects the truth of our need for safeguards, checks, and balances. Many organizations are building systems using zero trust architecture principles because it is necessary and wise. Zero trust architecture is what helps provide us humans with the ability to trust a system of interconnected computers.

While that's great from a technology perspective, we cannot program, configure, or architect trust into humans. It doesn't work that way. Trust is something that is cultivated and protected, resulting in a trustworthy character that is sustainable even in difficulty. We work in a human business, and no matter how many technical safety measures and verifications are in place, there is no such thing as a secure architecture without *people* we can trust.

Every good relationship we have is built in part on the currency of trust. Our relationship with our spouse or partner is built on mutual trust. Our relationship with our parents when we were teenagers probably waxed and waned depending on the amount of trust they placed in us. Our relationship with our supervisor at work is built on trust. Great teams are built on trust. Can you think of a significant relationship in your life that doesn't rest on the foundation of trust in some form or fashion?

Researcher John Gottman investigated the quality of trust to discover that it is the number-one quality people desire in a partner. He found that "trust" was one of the most searched for keywords on Amazon for books, and it was one of the most used words in the English language. Gottman's research reveals the importance of trust in relationships, communities, and even cultures.[12] Trust is a key element to the entirety of all our lives.

Trust Is the Currency of Cybersecurity

The problems we face in cybersecurity are principally human problems. While technology can help, the solutions in cybersecurity are principally human solutions. It is human beings who hold the keys to the most sensitive financial and healthcare data of ordinary people. It is humans who hold the keys to the most sensitive defense and military data of our governments. With this access and control comes tremendous responsibility. We *must* be able to trust them. As such, there is nothing more central to the cybersecurity profession than trust. Cybersecurity leaders and professionals *must* be trustworthy.

Trust is key to the logistics, to operations, and to the cybersecurity programs—the very hardwiring of the entire cyber world. Everything we can do on a computer requires trust. Consider what we take for granted. When we log in, we trust that the system admin won't capture our password. When we boot up our computer, we trust untold thousands of nameless, faceless people who designed the chips, fabricated them, integrated the hardware, wrote the firmware, designed the OS, and developed mountains of other software. Beyond our computer, trust is baked into the network, the servers, the APIs, and the cloud systems we interact with. Almost every online transaction we engage in requires us to trust thousands or tens of thousands of nameless people we will never meet. While zero-trust architectures work to provide some level of assurance, bad actors at multiple levels of software, hardware, and networking systems have a multitude of opportunities to take advantage of our trust.

The implicit trust we have in modern computing is astonishing.

However, cybersecurity is principally about people. We must be able to trust the ground-level cybersecurity operators and cybersecurity leaders.

How Trust Is Built

As we argued in the previous chapter, human beings have a zero-day vulnerability, meaning that people are inherently imperfect. We all make mistakes and bad decisions. Building trust and credibility have nothing to do with being perfect. Instead, it has everything to do with honesty, transparency, and accountability. These are the essentials to build, maintain, and, when needed, restore trust.

Think of building trust like opening and adding to a retirement account. You begin with an initial investment, normally quite small. If you add to the account using payroll deductions, you make incremental contributions on a regular basis. The early years of a retirement account are good and necessary, but they mark only a beginning. It is only over a long period of time that the compounding effect of incremental contributions and wise investment strategies can provide something truly meaningful.

Consider the reasons that we trust people with whom we have some sort of relationship. It begins with honesty. We increasingly trust people as they build a history of being truthful over a period of time. We look for actions to follow words. Trust grows when there is consistency between words and actions. The people who are most deeply trusted are those who have demonstrated a long consistency in the same direction.

Since people are imperfect, trust can also be damaged. In the worst situations, trust can be destroyed. Rebuilding trust is hard work. It requires ownership of the mistake or bad action, transparency, and an appropriate measure of accountability. It does *not* involve shifting blame, rejecting responsibility, or sweet-talking those who've been harmed. While rebuilding trust is hard work, it is essential to move forward in any relationship, whether at work or in our personal life.

Like the retirement account we discussed earlier, in every relationship you have, you have a nonmonetary but incredibly valuable relationship account. Trust is the credit to these relationship accounts. We all have an account with each person we know and interact with. In our professional settings, these are our co-workers, supervisors, shareholders, customers, and vendors. It's a wide group of people. Take a minute to consider two or three important relationships in your life. Is the trust account in a good place? Does it have a healthy balance? Is it low? What can you do to restore it?

When Things Go Bad

When you mishandle an interaction with a co-worker, mess up an audit, miss a vulnerability, accidentally ruin some evidence, or misread a possible breach, you are going to lose some credit. But you can mitigate how much "trust credit" you lose by being honest and accountable. If you mess up and report it to your management, they may be hesitant to let you jump right back into that task for a while, but if you lie about it or cover it up, you may *never* recover that trust. If you have been dishonest with your spouse or a friend, you need to set that account right by sharing the truth, even though it will hurt. It may be difficult in the short term, but over time, you may restore a healthy level of trust.

As important as our individual relationships are, there are also organizational concerns regarding trust. Is your organization/company trusted? How about its leadership? What happens if something damages that trust? There may be a situation where the mistake of one or more individuals impacts how customers, employees, and/or other shareholders view the organization. In the same way an individual needs to own mistakes, an organization needs to be honest, transparent, and implement an appropriate measure of accountability. Organizational trust, like trust between individuals, *can* be repaired and restored. But be careful not to under-assess the amount of work that needs to be done to win it back.

Building Trust Requires Courage

Courage is not a commonly observed trait. Yet, maintaining and growing trust requires courage. Unfortunately, there are many examples of how a *lack of courage* undermines trust. One such tragic example is found in the story of the famous American football coach Joe Paterno.

Coach Paterno was the head men's football coach at Penn State University from 1966 until 2011. In his 46 years as head coach at State, he amassed an NCAA record of 409 victories and remains the winningest coach in the history of Division I college football. He was revered as an all-time great. But in 2012, the statue of Coach Paterno that stood proudly outside the Penn State football stadium that holds

106,000 people each Saturday in the fall was unceremoniously removed. Coach Paterno's career ended when he was dismissed from the team in November 2011. He passed away 46 days later. What went so wrong for Paterno's career to end so badly?

Paterno was found *guilty of remaining silent* in the face of wrongdoing. One of his assistant coaches was convicted on 45 counts of sexual abuse of young boys, and Paterno was aware of the abuse but did not contact law enforcement authorities. A subsequent investigation by former FBI director Louis Freeh concluded that Paterno's actions "failed to protect against a child sexual predator harming children for over a decade." He chose to protect the success of his program over doing what was right. He chose self-preservation over the truth. In the end, his choice was anything but self-preservation. Paterno's entire career and legacy were shattered over his decision not to speak up about these terrible abuses. Such squandering of trust is tragic.

Please do not dismiss the Paterno example because you say to yourself that you would never allow children to be abused or placate yourself by thinking you would never do something that egregious. The cybersecurity profession is filled with stories of wrongdoing taking place inside organizations where no one was courageous enough to speak up or take action. As leaders and educators in the field of cybersecurity, we know that young professionals are faced regularly with situations where an ethical choice should take precedence over the discomfort of speaking up.

These aren't always major decisions. In fact, many of them are not. You may have come face-to-face with one recently. For example, what if your company passes a cybersecurity audit, but you're pretty certain that it shouldn't have? We see this happen rather often—the auditors might miss some massive vulnerabilities or come to improper conclusions about the organization's cybersecurity stance. Sometimes, the cybersecurity team knows the organization should not have passed the audit. What if you go to your supervisor to report that the auditors missed significant vulnerabilities but you are ignored by management? How will it affect your career if you speak up for what you believe to be true?

As we mentioned in Chapter 4, "'Zero-Day' Humanity and Accountability," we encourage you to exercise great wisdom in considering whether to go around your direct supervisor. Before doing so, we recommend that you seek the counsel of a person you can trust who can be an objective third party and who is not directly in your line of reporting relationships. We don't think there is a single answer for these situations, and we think a mentor, thoughtful colleague, or experienced friend can help.

Demonstrating a measure of courage in something relatively small will likely have the effect of giving you the confidence to do so again at a later point. Like most traits or skills, we need to practice to get better. We need to build our courage "muscle" to make it stronger. As you exercise this muscle, you will find yourself becoming more comfortable exercising courage, and you will likely be willing to be courageous on matters of greater significance.

Why does courage matter? Because as cybersecurity professionals and leaders, we are entrusted with some of the most sensitive data and information a person can possess. It is our charge to be the safeguard for that information. It is our challenge and privilege to protect that which could be vulnerable. Everything you do in cybersecurity—big or small—is making things either more secure or less. Courage is absolutely critical if trust is going to grow and thrive.

The Role of Leadership in Building a Culture of Trust

One of the challenges of today's cybersecurity work environment is the gap between how quickly young practitioners gain the necessary skills to advance in their career and how important it is for them to demonstrate the ethics and character necessary to be trusted with their responsibilities. In an industry that is projected to be short more than a million workers in the United States alone, it is difficult to create systems and avenues for rising professionals to demonstrate or even learn the trust that is a prerequisite for certain positions that are responsible for sensitive and important data.

Perhaps more than ever, it is incumbent upon leaders in cybersecurity to play an important role in forming and developing an ethical decision-making framework for their employees and students. We can no longer make assumptions about the ethical standards of our hires. It is paramount that leaders lead by example on ethics, which may be a new concept for some. Cybersecurity leaders have the potential to build a culture of ethics and trust if they are observed by others to make decisions carefully, taking the ethical implications of their decisions into account. Do not forget that your employees, your clients, your students, and your colleagues are watching—they are *always* watching. While this may be sobering, it's good to remember. This reality will serve to help you be accountable to the culture you aspire to build.

Beyond good modeling, the cybersecurity leader also needs to articulate explicitly and out loud that ethical decision-making is essential. Beyond saying it out loud, it must be taught and practiced. Like any good habit, practice is at the core of success.

Our friend Olivia remembers her job at a shoe store, which has served as a great reminder of the significance and benefit of building trust with her supervisor. The first day on the job, she arrived excited to sell shoes, but she recalls that her boss, Reggie, sent her to the back with an experienced employee who showed her how to stock shoes and do inventory. The first three weeks on the job, Olivia was directed to do various menial tasks in the back of the store with the oversight of seasoned employees who would check her progress. Olivia recounts that each day, she showed up on time for work and faithfully completed the tasks given to her by her manager. With punctuality and each completed task, she was gaining trust. It was a full month of work before Olivia proved she knew enough about the different shoe brands on the floor and was "finally" allowed to work directly with customers. It was six months into the job when she began to use the cash register. A year and a half later, Olivia was promoted to assistant manager. The merits of that promotion were earned day-in and day-out by her reliability. She showed up on time. She did what she was told. She was honest. Olivia describes with affection all she learned from that experience and how the promotion carried her through college where she would earn her degree and go to work in the cybersecurity profession.

We encourage you to be reflective and thoughtful about how quickly you hand over the keys to the company sports car to your newly hired drivers. Have a well-thought-out, thorough system for your new hires like Olivia's boss at the shoe store. Pay attention to how your people handle the smaller tasks before you give them bigger ones.

Some leaders we know approach trust with an all-or-nothing mentality. These leaders either don't trust anyone or trust everyone. We think neither is a good option. Instead, we urge you to teach, mentor, and build a system of accruing trust on an individual-by-individual basis into your leadership toolbox. The goal, of course, is to have the type of practitioners and subordinate leaders around you that are faithfully executing the job the way it is supposed to be done, with your mutual trust accruing in your employees and your own accounts. But remember, neither you nor your leadership will ever be perfect. No matter what system you have in place for people to earn your trust, it will be violated on occasion.

A friendly reminder: teaching trust or being trustworthy doesn't make the headlines. Yet, we consider trust and trustworthiness to be at the heart of the cybersecurity profession. You could argue this is true of any profession, and we would agree. But, trust is especially foundational in cybersecurity, given the immense importance of computing systems and sensitive data in our world and the need to keep them secure. In our combined decades of leadership experience, our perception of a prospective employee's trustworthiness is the number-one quality we look for in hiring.

Leaders also need to exercise trust by placing it in others. Many leaders are ineffective because they are unwilling to trust those around them. A leader unwilling to trust good, proven, trustworthy employees will create a host of challenges, not the least of which is micromanagement. We see micromanagement as a lose-lose proposition. Effective leaders with competent and able employees can step away from their organizations for a period, and things continue to run smoothly. This is partly because employees have been empowered to achieve their goals and are trusted to do so.

A Checklist for Building Trust

Let's take a closer look at some practical strategies that can help you build a strong foundation of trust at work. Like everything else in this book, building trust is a skill that we can work at and improve. Just as we can become better cybersecurity analysts, better communicators, and better leaders, we can learn to embrace the kind of practices that grow and nurture trust.

- **Be truthful.** Trust requires us to be truthful. This means telling the truth even when it doesn't benefit you personally or professionally, or doesn't benefit your organization. We covered this in the previous chapter when we talked about accountability and the fact that we all make mistakes. It means that we never shade or hide the full truth. If you have discovered a breach, then disclose it. If you have discovered a vulnerability in code that is now in production, rather than keep your fingers crossed and hope no one notices, go to leadership or a project manager and reveal it.

- **Deliver bad news quickly.** Bad news is not like wine; it does not get better with time. You may discover that one of your systems has been infected with malware. Maybe that system has no sensitive data. Rather than ignore it, deliver the news quickly. This might mean that you make sure to follow your organization's guidelines regarding the urgency of various cybersecurity vulnerabilities or incidents. As we have noted, even a short delay can mean a much bigger data loss. No one likes to be the bearer of bad news, but it is every bit as important as delivering good news.

- **Be transparent with discretion.** Sometimes, for reasons of safety and propriety, you need to avoid disclosing certain details because they could hurt individuals or fly in the face of other ethical principles (such as harming an individual's privacy, a topic we'll discuss in detail in Chapter 9, "It's None of Your Business"). For example, if your organization has been hacked and you need to let customers and the public know, you must also know which details can be provided publicly and which information is appropriate to hold back. You don't want to replicate, cause unnecessary panic, or even tip off other attackers about potential vulnerabilities. Discretion with transparency means that honesty and confession need to go hand in hand with wisdom. Exercise discernment before you choose to be a whistleblower by taking your concerns to the people inside your organization who may be able to fix the issue. Practicing transparency with discretion requires that we have mentors and people in our lives to whom we can ask hard questions. We also need to remember we are beholden to a higher ethical standard than our loyalty to a company or organization.

- **Be a person of your word.** When we say we will complete a task, then we need to complete it. When we say we will be at work on time, we must do everything we can to show up on time. Being a person of your word is not trite. It is essential to being trusted and will build up credits in your trust accounts. Honor your contracts, live up to your commitments, and hold fast to being honest in your dealings. This means being truthful with yourself and others. It may mean coming to your supervisor and asking for more time on a project so it is done right rather than meeting the deadline and leaving possible vulnerabilities in the program. It means making promises in marketing that can be fulfilled. Being a person of your word is foundational in accruing trust. No matter how well-intentioned we are when we over-promise, when we under-deliver, we undermine the very trust we are working hard to establish. Both as practitioners and as leaders, we need to do what we say we will do.

> ## Code-Critical Application
> Read the following case study and answer the questions applying what you have learned in this chapter.

Case Study: A Matter of Trust and Data Breaches

Brittany received a phone call from a newspaper reporter who indicated that her organization, a fitness company with thousands of gym locations across the country had suffered a breach. Of course, it wasn't just any newspaper; it was the tech reporter for the *Times*, a national publication sitting at the checkout line of every coffee house and on the newsfeed of pretty much every smartphone in America. As the communications director, she immediately did a three-way call with Sam, the chief information security officer (CISO), to verify the story with the reporter. Sam was adamant that the reporter was wrong until the tech reporter began to share some of the sensitive information released in the attack. Credit card numbers connected to more than 100,000 gym memberships had been exposed online in the last 24 hours. The two got off the phone with the *Times* and began to go through their breach procedures. Sam called his team and set the internal investigation rolling. They called their support center to get as much data as they could on the breach. The two then immediately walked up to the fourth-floor office of the company chief executive officer (CEO) and founder, Mike, to deliver the grim news.

Mike had built his fitness organization from the ground up and was still involved in the day-to-day decisions of the national brand. He was also a fitness guru and knew that handling cybersecurity issues was not in his skill set. Sam presented the quickly evolving investigation with the internal security team (which was only four employees) and their contracted third-party security firm. They examined various logs and did some quick threat hunting to try to discover the attacker's presence in their environment. Of course, each area presented its own challenges, but in a stroke of luck, they found the breach point in the company's new application that was designed by a third party and launched six months ago.

The company markets itself as "the most trusted name in fitness," and everyone in the C-suite board room meeting that day was committed to that foundational company belief. As the leader of the organization, Mike reminded his leadership team that, when things get difficult, the culture of the company they discussed all the time would take over. In a meeting with the third-party security firm and all the members of the company leadership team, they discussed how to move forward and reestablish trust with their consumers. The legal team cautioned restraint in disclosing the breach. The third-party security firm believed that they should hold off on informing the public until the extent of the breach was fully investigated. The chief financial officer (CFO), Amy, proposed that they launch an internal investigation and respond to the forthcoming *Times* story by saying that they are "looking into the problem." The application developer was concerned that they would lose market share if they chose to take down the fitness application completely. Most of the leadership team spoke out against public disclosure of the breach, but Mike pushed the issue. He wanted to be fully transparent with the public without divulging anything that would encourage another attack or empower another breach.

The security team and consultants first decided what elements of the breach could safely be disclosed in their initial public announcement. Mike then consulted with the board of directors, and together, they made the difficult decision to take down the application until it could be deemed secure. They had learned that the *Times* would run the story about the data breach in their evening digital news cycle, and it would be included in the print edition the following morning. Mike was passionate that the company's loyal consumers learn about the stolen data first from the company itself (instead of the newspaper), so the communications team went to work with the security team and legal counsel to craft a press release to go out before 4 p.m. to the media and the company's clients across the country.

In the months that followed, the fitness company's stock dipped significantly, and they lost customers throughout the third quarter, as they worked to recover from the data breach and the subsequent fallout. They lost 25% of their subscribers to the company's fitness application, but analytics showed that week by week, they were slowly recovering that subscription loss through new promotions and discounts. In several audits of the company's customers, the brand retained high marks on value and consumer confidence despite the national media coverage of the data breach. The culture of the company as the "most trusted brand in fitness" seemed to indeed take over, and by the fourth quarter, earnings had returned to pre-breach levels. The new application, by all accounts, was more secure than it was in the initial launch. The breach was eventually traced to a design flaw in the application, and the third-party application development firm had their contract canceled. Mike, Brittany, Sam, and the rest of the organization learned the value of being trustworthy, but it came at a cost.

Critical Application Questions

What are some of the risks the fitness company ran into by adopting the policy of full disclosure? How would you advise Mike, the CEO, differently?

What do the company's actions do to encourage consumer trust?

Do you agree with a disclosure policy? Is it correct to take the application down until it is deemed secure? What could have been done differently?

How do the actions of leadership in this scenario inspire trust?

Can you think of some examples of companies that handled a breach differently? How did it impact your trust in them?

If you are an industry practitioner and have experienced a similar situation, explain how it was handled by your superiors. Did you agree with their course of action?

What are some day-to-day actions that managers and leaders can take to build trust and inspire a culture that is prepared for the types of crises presented in this case study?

How are the principles of trust we have discussed in the chapter handled by each of the characters in this scene (such as Brittany, the communications director; Sam, the CISO; and Mike, the CEO)?

Does your organization have written incident response procedures for a cybersecurity incident? If so, have you read them? What do they say about decision-making and communication during a breach?

Do you have any recommendations for your own organization about improvements to your incident response procedures based on the case studies in this book or other things you've learned?

Does your organization have a culture of trust, honesty, and open communication that encourages candid conversations about concerns or mistakes?

6

There Is Strength in the Pack

"I will not be a lone wolf but will instead work collaboratively with my peers and superiors."
> – The Cybersecurity Code of Honor

"Alone we can do so little; together we can do so much."
> – Helen Keller

"It is the long history of humankind (and animal kind, too) that those who learned to collaborate and improvise most effectively have prevailed."
> – Charles Darwin

Jonah was a rising junior cybersecurity analyst at a New York City investment firm. He had graduated from one of the top cybersecurity university programs in the United States a year ago and was already taking on new initiatives with responsibilities far beyond his years at the firm. Even the chief information security officer (CISO) at the firm, Shelby, was taking notice of Jonah's work. Jonah operated on a team with three other security specialists who were seasoned professionals: Tom was a security analyst with eight years of experience; Selah was the current team leader, a former developer who had been working in cybersecurity for more than a decade; and, finally, there was his friend Moses, who had come to the firm after serving in a cybersecurity role in the U.S. armed forces. It was a competent team with good leadership that generally worked well together. Rumor had it that Jonah was up for a review and likely promotion to team leader in the coming weeks.

But the following Monday found Jonah sitting in his CISO's office early in the morning for an urgent meeting. This face-to-face talk wasn't about an expected promotion. In fact, Jonah's boss was in a somber mood. Shelby informed Jonah that he had violated several of the organization's security policies and procedures, and there was no way around a termination. Of course, Jonah presented his case and tried to explain his intent, but it didn't matter—he couldn't argue the facts. The organization had just suffered a terrible breach that was still unfolding and proving very costly. It was also a breach that could have been contained if Jonah had simply gone to his team instead of trying to handle it on his own.

On Friday of the previous week, just after 1 p.m., Jonah identified a malware alert and began to dig into its cause. He quickly diagnosed it as a minor malware infection of a seemingly unimportant workstation. With a sure promotion upcoming, the rising star decided that he would handle this on his own rather than alerting his team. It was a decision he made quickly and without much reflection. He was eager to impress his superiors. He investigated the issue by looking up the specific variant of malware on the Internet. He found a couple of descriptions of it, but they were contradictory, confusing Jonah for just a bit. Still, he moved forward to fix the situation without help. He was able to pinpoint and eradicate the malware with ease, and the entire case seemed to wrap up quickly. He considered that the resolution came almost too quickly, but he chalked it up to his proficiency as an analyst. He marked the matter resolved and closed out his week by writing up a short status report on what he accomplished. Absentmindedly, he didn't mention the small malware incident in his report that he emailed to his team leader, Selah, and his CISO, Shelby.

By Monday morning, the entire IT department, from security to development, was in five-alarm crisis mode. The "small infection" Jonah had marked resolved was far from it. In his inexperience, Jonah had failed to investigate other areas of the system that were connected to the issue. He thought he had contained it by removing one file. But in his haste, he had left a much larger set of malicious files on the system, which allowed a group of cybercriminals from Eastern Europe to move laterally to compromise other systems while hunting for sensitive data about financial customers. Ultimately, data from more than six million of the institution's clients had been stolen.

So, rather than the anticipated promotion, Jonah was going to be terminated. The CISO would later use Jonah's mistake in a talk at a security conference to point out the necessity of being a team player in the cybersecurity field. Jonah excelled in his specific area as an analyst, but he couldn't see the more comprehensive picture that someone more experienced with different specializations may have noticed. If he simply would have taken the case to another team member to verify his assessment, the breach could have been identified as much bigger than he assessed, and the eradication could have been done much more thoroughly. Jonah was doing something we are all tempted to do from time to time. He was going at it alone. He was doing all the work because he wanted the individual accolades. In the process, he inadvertently violated the company policies and procedures associated with even seemingly small malware infections, which should have been logged and reviewed by others on the team. Even if a promotion had not been anticipated in Jonah's case, the temptation to handle a breach on your own is still significant.

Jonah's situation is not uncommon in our industry. We've detailed before how we spend much of our time operating independently behind keyboards and screens. We often receive recognition for our skill set and our ingenuity as *individuals*. But at the end of the day, cybersecurity requires a team-first mindset. Our industry has become so specialized and complex that no one person can manage the vast scope and intricacy of the work alone.

We've addressed the truth that cybersecurity problems are human problems and that we all deal with our own human zero-day vulnerability that can be mitigated only by leaning on each other. Wisdom from Rudyard Kipling's *Jungle Book*, "For the strength of the pack is the wolf, and the strength of the wolf is the pack," seems to fit well in our approach to cybersecurity. There is strength in numbers. We need other people to be successful, which begins with a healthy level of self-awareness, humility, and relationship-building.

No Room for Know-it-Alls

No one likes a know-it-all. To most people, a know-it-all comes across as unlikable. Unfortunately, there are larger problems with know-it-alls than likability. It begins with the need for heightened self-awareness. Think of the first steps in 12-step recovery programs: they begin with the admission of not having all the answers. This self-awareness is essential for cybersecurity practitioners and leaders. But this humility must run deeper than a simple admission of our own limitations. We must constantly and actively remind ourselves that we *do not and will not* have all the answers. We must adopt the mindset and practice of always questioning assumptions and being intentional to seek out the wisdom of others.

A prominent business leader in our community once remarked to us over dinner about the qualities he looks for when he hires managers. His approach is that *what they know* isn't always as important as what they *want* to know. He explained that if he talks with a potential manager who believes they know everything already, he would bet on failure in the long run. Why? Because if you don't believe you can learn from others, you won't be willing to lean into their strengths. Professional success requires the humility to know that other people are necessary to solve problems and achieve the collective goals of your security team.

As a leader, you might consider the practice of assigning teams of two people to work together on a project, especially in the areas of penetration testing and incident handling. Such an approach not only fosters cross-training, it also provides accountability and verification. If you are working in the C-suite in a commercial organization, you likely have the option of gaining wise counsel from some combination of members of your board of directors, CEO, and peers in senior leadership.

As a practitioner, stay hungry to learn from others. As the field of cybersecurity becomes more and more specialized, it has become virtually impossible for one person to know everything they need to know to get the overall job done. Not having all the answers is not a weakness. *Instead, being able to ask questions and seek the input and perspectives of others is a tremendous strength.*

We encourage practitioners to find ways to share their day-in and day-out decisions with members of their team. In the case of Jonah, from the start of this chapter, a simple phone call or chat session with one of his teammates to help him weigh in on that specific malware could have mitigated a disastrous situation. The old wisdom is true: pride comes before the fall. Put another way, there are two kinds of cybersecurity professionals: those who are humble and those who are about to be humbled. We all make mistakes and misjudgments. We need to make sure they aren't a result of complacency, arrogance, or the false assumption that we know it all. Whether you lead or are on the front lines, there is no room for know-it-alls. Seek the help of others.

Making Informed Ethical Decisions with Input

You will make better ethical decisions if you consult with trusted individuals on your team and in your life. You must use discretion and respect confidentiality agreements. Yet, when an ethical dilemma arises, it is wise to bounce ideas, concerns, and possible plans of action off of colleagues on your team or those in leadership. If you are in leadership, trusted people who report to you can be invaluable sounding boards for making better decisions. Receiving the counsel of others will almost certainly identify issues and considerations you had not taken into account or angles that may even surprise you.

Both of us rely heavily on the wise counsel of friends, peers, and people who report to us to help keep us on the right path. Such advice can be especially helpful if the folks you seek are grounded in a known, well-understood, shared ethical framework, such as the Cybersecurity Code of Honor. In a way, these advisors are like a garden that you need to carefully plant and painstakingly tend to, which will yield abundant harvests for you over time. You also need to give back, helping others in your circle of advisors work through their own ethical dilemmas.

Why Teamwork Really Does Make the Dream Work

Many cyber leaders and practitioners put their heads down and try to plow through difficult problems alone rather than interact collaboratively. To change this dynamic, thought-leading organizations establish policies, processes, checks, and balances to compel and reward collaborative work. The silo mentality is natural, so it requires intentional leadership, structures, and decisions to break down the mindset that naturally wants to emerge. At Paul's college, we make sure that significant decisions are always made collaboratively. And at Ed's firm, there are strategies to ensure that every project we take on is a shared project. This is neither pollyannish nor an inefficient approach to work or management. It also isn't specific to cybersecurity. It is a necessity for long-term success.

Let's step outside the cybersecurity space and examine some of the superior work done in teams.

Even in the most individual of sports like tennis, you will often hear Wimbledon tournament winners recognize their team after a victory. No matter how elite the individual athlete, they understand their trainers, their nutritionists, and even their sponsors have helped enable their accomplishments. In a culture that celebrates individual success, we are remiss to ignore the reality that no achievement is truly accomplished alone. No matter how dominant an athlete Michael Jordan was on a basketball court; he couldn't have won six NBA championships without Chicago Bulls teammates like Scottie Pippin, Horace Grant, and Steve Kerr or a coach like Phil Jackson. As brilliant a vocalist as Ella Fitzgerald was, she worked with elite musicians and songwriters to deliver some of her most memorable performances. As revered as Steve Jobs is for driving innovation in the tech world, he still needed Woz, Hartmut Esslinger, and Jony Ive to help him create an engineering and design aesthetic that set Apple apart for decades.

Whatever we believe about success, it is not a lone-wolf endeavor. Bestselling author Malcolm Gladwell, who has studied success in many areas of life, points out that "Success is not a function of individual talent. It's the steady accumulation of advantages. It's bound up in so many other broader circumstantial, environmental, historical, and cultural factors." As leaders and team members, we contribute to creating the environment and culture for high achievement to germinate. Working in a team environment can create a level of joy, healthy collaboration, and even friendly competition that produces better results. Teamwork accentuates shared experience, which builds community and contributes to higher levels of job satisfaction. Collaborative work surrounds us with people who bring different perspectives and experiences to each task, creating a more informed, well-rounded foundation for critical thinking, decision-making, and better ethical choices.

Managers and leaders sometimes can be the ones most tempted to retreat to the silo space at work. For some, the higher one rises in leadership, the less open they are to collaboration. There are practical reasons for this. Leaders can operate on their own out of a sense of self-preservation. Leaders often have put in long hours to rise to their level and generally want to protect it. They can also default to the idea that it's simply easier and faster to just do it alone, which can be frequently true. Making tough decisions also lends itself to a bit of isolation in leadership. These tendencies of self-insulation and isolation for people in leadership happen naturally unless we are intentional and proactive. The higher you climb, the less populated that altitude will be. It is not uncommon for CEOs to lack mentors and friends, which also can lead to isolated decision-making. Your leadership must include collaboration for long-term success.

The higher you rise in leadership, and the more responsibility you are given, the greater the need to lean into others and build trust with the team around you. This may require a mindset shift that Jim Collins explains so well in his book *Good to Great*: "Good to great leaders never want to become larger-than-life heroes. They never aspired to be put on a pedestal or become unreachable icons." As leaders, we *want* people around us who are given permission to ask us tough questions and offer perspectives that we have not considered.

While you don't always need to argue, thought-provoking conversations with good challenges and critical thinking are vital for success. If we are or become complacent or smug in our standing or success, we will tend to surround ourselves with people who tell us what we want to hear. We will carve out spaces where we can operate alone and avoid the give-and-take of critical thinking. The higher we rise, the more important it becomes to build trustworthy teams, hire trustworthy people, and foster trustworthy mentors. We must be able to lean on others. Although it is true that top leadership is often lonely, that does not mean it must or should be for lone wolves.

The rapid expansion of the cybersecurity field and the subsequent hyper-specialization of our work means no single person can have the breadth of expertise and understanding required to manage everything. This applies to leaders as well as practitioners. Here is an illustration of how expansion in specific expertise necessitates collaboration in business: Suppose Ann is an analyst at a company and is an expert at doing host forensics. There is a high probability she will look at various network artifacts beyond the host to analyze an investigation properly. This means Ann will need the help of a network forensics specialist to figure out the full scope of an investigation. In our opening illustration about Jonah, he likely violated his firm's procedures when an incident occurred that would have required him to collaborate or inform a team member who specialized in another area. If you are in leadership, it is helpful to build teams with varying skill sets. If you are a practitioner, it is critical for you to lean on the expertise of other members of your team and be available to offer your specialized skill set to others when necessary.

When Collaboration Breaks Down—Seeking Allies in Your Organization

Sometimes collaboration and open communication break down. We've seen numerous examples where someone in an organization notices something that doesn't seem quite right from an ethical perspective. They consult with their peers and maybe even their superiors and are told to ignore it. Or perhaps the response is a little softer and gentler—a disarming, kind "Pay no attention to that man behind the curtain," as the Wizard of Oz said to Dorothy and her gang. Or sometimes, peers or management don't even respond at all to issues that an employee highlights. You get the silent treatment. What do you do then? Are you prepared to go up the management chain or seek help from elsewhere in the organization? It's a common ethical question that comes up frequently in our classes on cybersecurity.

Situations like this illustrate the value of security practitioners having a solid relationship with people in your company outside of your direct reporting line but higher in management in the organization. Perhaps you know someone in the C-suite, or you might have an acquaintance in your legal department. Perhaps you know a manager in the audit team. Maybe you know someone in HR that you can turn to for advice. If you don't know folks from these different groups, seek out and cultivate such relationships. With friends and allies like these, you'll have some alternatives for getting advice on sticky ethical situations you may encounter. Alternatively, some larger organizations have special hotlines or people dedicated to helping employees address such concerns, especially issues associated with ethics and organizational integrity. Find out if your organization does and learn the guidelines for requesting such assistance.

Of course, if you choose to go outside of your normal reporting structure to point out a potential ethical lapse, there could be serious consequences. By doing so, you may burn one or more bridges, so you want to make sure you consult with your supervisor and potentially peers to ensure you are properly understanding and interpreting the facts of the situation. Also, it *may* be worthwhile to indicate to your boss or peers that you are considering calling someone in your organization outside of your group for their advice. This may help to get their attention, but it could also backfire, drawing ire and negative consequences for you, and, of course, your boss just might tell you not to do it. These are indeed complex, murky, and potentially dangerous waters, but they are important. Consider this carefully, and you may even want to bounce some ideas off of a mentor you have in or outside of your organization, respecting nondisclosure agreements, of course.

The Power of Mentors

One of the primary ways we develop as professionals and stay away from the silo, or lone-wolf mentality, is by engaging teachers and mentors. Indeed, one of the best things you can do to help improve your ethical decision-making overall is to establish a relationship with one or more trustworthy, wise mentors. For such mentor relationships to work, the process must be proactive and intentional. It is much easier to focus on your work and keep your own counsel. We think there's a better way, which involves having relationships with people to whom you can turn to with your ethical, technical, career-specific, and even relationship questions.

A good mentor will provide valuable insight into what really matters in your life and career while moving you toward a strategic balance of competing influences. A good mentor can also be a source of accountability as you face ethical dilemmas in your work. Mentors can be invaluable to your development as a professional and as a person.

Mentors have played a huge role both in our careers and in our personal lives. They mean so much to us that we want to take a minute to tell you about two of them who have made profound impacts on us, respectively.

Tom Hammon was the area director of an organization called Young Life when Paul was a student at the University of Cincinnati. In his role as a volunteer leader with Young Life, Paul recounts how Tom regularly met him, trained him, and invested in their relationship, which allowed them to discuss anything and everything. One particular conversation was catalytic and ultimately influenced Paul to pursue being a college president. To this day, more than 40 years later, Paul still credits his mentor's encouragement and affirmation for emboldening him to follow career avenues that he would not have been confident enough to otherwise seek.

Alan Paller was Ed's most influential mentor. Ed carefully listened to Alan's advice, making sure to ask good questions and following through by implementing what he learned from Alan into his career and family life. While Alan's mentorship of Ed began specifically with cybersecurity industry advice, over the years, it grew into broader "how to run a business" advice and finally to relationship and family advice, which was life-changing for Ed.

We can trace the influence of these and other mentors in our lives and careers that led the two of us into positions where we can collaborate on this book and be part of introducing the Cybersecurity Code of Honor to the World.

It is important for you to seek out those who are wiser and more advanced in their journey because the breadth and depth of their experiences will prove to be invaluable. These are people who can ask good questions, and both encourage and challenge you in a healthy way. These are people who can help you become the best version of yourself—someone with whom you can be honest and to whom you are willing to be accountable, a person who can help you maintain your sense of ethical integrity as you navigate your career.

Finding mentors is an *intentional* process that requires effort. We offer a couple guidelines for identifying and developing a working relationship with someone who might be a good mentor.

Step #1: Identify who you want as a mentor. A mentor has more wisdom and/or years of experience than you have. It is someone who doesn't see you as a competitor for clients or promotions or feels threatened by you professionally. While your supervisor may have a mentoring role in your professional development, we encourage you to find someone outside of that direct-report relationship. If you work in cybersecurity, try to find someone who is at least five years your senior in the industry. A mentor is also someone you admire for the right reasons—someone you have observed following the ethics and principles included in the Cybersecurity Code of Honor. You want someone who is wise and deserves your respect.

Mentors can be specific to one area. Maybe you can find a mentor in a specific technical area, such as software development, and then another mentor who is great at managing people. A mentor does not need to be limited to your professional life. A mentor can also provide perspective and wisdom regarding marriage, parenting, and/or your personal health.

Step #2: Make it easy for the mentor. Reach out to them to determine a time and location that will work best for them. If they can meet only before work, then ask to buy them coffee at 6:45 a.m. somewhere convenient for them. You may have to go out of your way to meet them at their office for 20 minutes in between meetings. Remember, these people have the wisdom you want, so be thoughtful not to make inconvenient requests of them. A chief financial officer (CFO) friend commented that a young auditing professional asked him if he would be willing to be a mentor and then followed up by sending a rather demanding meeting request. Needless to say, those demanding requests didn't work out well for him. Every year, Ed gets a few mentorship requests from people in the industry. Ed is happy to help where he can, but he's often only available at 6:30 or 7 a.m. Several times, would-be mentees have sighed and proclaimed, "That's just too early for me!" We do hope they found other mentors, but Ed feels sad when issues like these get in the way of solid mentor relationships.

Step #3: Follow through on your mentor's advice. Remember, if these people are good enough to offer you their time and be a mentor, you should be attentive, take notes, and follow through. Whenever you meet with a mentor, especially a professional mentor, you should come to the meeting prepared with good questions to ask. It is OK to have a notebook and jot down what they say at times. Don't feel sheepish about it because it is not cheesy—it is smart and respectful. In most situations, it is important to reference and revisit at least some of the advice you receive from a mentor relationship. Remember, this isn't exactly a friendship, although it's great when those develop. If someone agrees to mentor you, they want to have a positive influence on your career or life. Communicate with them about how you are implementing their wisdom and advice in your life. Thanking them is a basic, essential courtesy, but follow-through is just as important.

Beware of Rattlesnakes

Success doesn't happen in a vacuum. No matter how hard you have worked to get where you are today, you didn't get here on your own. We need a team. We dare not try to do it on our own. Our friend Matt recalls flying out to Colorado Springs for business and being put up for a night on a property adjacent to the stunning Garden of the Gods geological formations. An avid runner, Matt woke early the next morning, laced up his running shoes and began to run up a beautiful nature trail just a few feet from the back entrance of the property. He explains that he wasn't quite 30 feet into his run when he rounded a corner to be stopped by a large, unmistakably clear sign at the narrowed entrance of the long nature trail. The sign read, "Beware of rattlesnakes. Do NOT hike alone." Our Midwestern friend explains how quickly he made a U-turn and promptly returned to the safety of his room and unlaced his running shoes, deciding he would opt for a rest day rather than risk coming face-to-face with a rattlesnake.

Experienced mountain climbers offer a similar sentiment about the dangers of going it alone. Climbing is technical, dangerous, and complicated. No matter how seasoned you may be as a climber, it isn't really a solo endeavor. As you plan for the expedition, you look for people whose strengths can complement your weaknesses. You look for younger people who may have higher fitness levels that will be helpful for certain stages of the climb. You look for older, wiser, and more experienced climbers who have navigated similar terrains. If you are fortunate, you will find people who have climbed that mountain before to go with you as well. You want to have guides who can help you navigate the weather patterns and changing conditions the mountain will bring at different altitudes. It is unwise to climb mountains alone. We aren't gearing up for a climb, but the perils of cybersecurity have real consequences. There are metaphorical rattlesnakes on the trails we hike. The threats in cybersecurity often emerge faster than we can imagine. To be the best we can be, we must lean into the strength of the pack. We really do need each other.

Code-Critical Application

Read the following case study and answer the questions applying what you have learned in this chapter.

Case Study: Graded on a Curve? The Security Audit Checkmark

Senior security managers at a national retail merchant, Sofia and Ron were walking to the parking lot, heading out for the off-site department meeting when the notification came through their phones from the lead auditor, Jalen, that they had passed the major security audit from a third-party IT audit firm. Sofia and Ron each led their own security teams and had worked at the company for more than five years. "That can't be right," Ron said to his co-manager.

The two jumped in the car to drive to the off-site planning meeting with their CISO, Gina, and the rest of their security team. The chief information officer (CIO) had scheduled their afternoon to plan several new initiatives to be completed by the close of the fiscal year. The board was forecasting the budget at next week's meeting and wanted specific objectives in place. The national retail merchant was rolling out a revamped consumer mobile app and online web presence at the end of the year, and all resources were being invested in these areas. The passing audit grade was the green light for a host of technical innovations that the security team would have to support.

After lunch at the meeting site in a private dining room, the CISO, Gina, congratulated her two security teams led by Ron and Sofia on passing the security audit. They all took a moment to open their computers and look through the report. The company passed with only minimal, superficial changes required, receiving a much coveted "satisfactory" rating on the cybersecurity audit. Gina explained that they could implement the changes rather quickly and would be given a clean bill of health. She said that they would be putting their resources toward the consumer-focused launch and wouldn't be revisiting the audit in the coming weeks. At this point in the meeting, several folks on the team started discussing the audit quite passionately.

Technical team members began to voice concern about how the auditors inexplicably missed several significant security issues. Ron spoke up in support of his staff and told Gina he didn't agree with the passing grade. He felt the auditors had graded the company on a curve. Members of Ron's team had concerns that the auditor overlooked three significant vulnerabilities. On the other hand, Sofia and most of her team felt that the company had done enough to pass the audit. They weren't worried and wanted to move on to the next project conversation. The room was divided. Finally, Sofia responded to Ron's concerns; if the auditors were hired to identify flaws and believed the company was secure, then why make their jobs more complicated and question it? After all, Sofia reminded the room that the company's goal is not security; it is truly innovative retail.

A heated argument broke out in the room, and Gina finally stepped in. She told the team they would take the next hour to review the audit and look at Ron's concerns. Gina had been with the company for 12 years. She was a seasoned leader and former penetration tester who had come to the security division working her way up to the CISO role. She had also hired Ron, a former programmer, and Sofia, an all-star hire from a renowned university cybersecurity program. She trusted both as team leaders and respected their opinions. The security group abandoned the planning meeting instead to review the audit.

After an hour of intense discussion, Gina made the call. The team was going to focus on the task they were given from their CIO, Brandon, to prioritize the goals for next quarter's application rollout. Ron was furious. He and several members of his team were certain that the audit was overlooking specific vulnerabilities that could hurt the organization and its customers. He followed Gina to her car and once again voiced his concern about the audit. Gina told him she would approach her superior, the CIO, about the issue the next morning.

The next morning, Gina called Ron into her office and informed him that the CIO, along with the leadership team, had been very direct in response to her questions about the audit. They had passed, and that was the end of the story. They were not to dedicate division resources to any issues surrounding the audit other than the minor tweaks and patches that had been recommended. In response to this news, Ron handed her his report detailing the vulnerabilities he felt had been overlooked in the audit. He explained his assessment that the company could be putting millions of consumers at risk. Gina lost patience with Ron and told him to drop his complaints and follow through with what he was supposed to accomplish. She said the company had bigger concerns and would reprimand him if he wasted any more time discussing the audit. Ron stormed out of the office.

Gina wasn't particularly concerned about his behavior. They had been through some very stressful situations together, and Ron's passionate response wasn't unusual. Sofia dropped by Gina's office later that day, and they discussed the report that Ron had compiled. Sofia agreed that Ron's view of the potential vulnerabilities was exaggerated. She also told Gina that Ron's home situation wasn't going well, and he was probably dealing with a lot of stress.

Ron returned to his office that day and went about his business. Several of the members of his team came by to voice their support for him standing up against the audit's findings. But they had their marching orders, right? After-hours that evening, Ron pulled up his audit research from the night before and the potential vulnerabilities. He poured over his analytics again and just shook his head. There were three major issues that could lead to a breach. The team had discussed each earlier in the year and the audit simply overlooked them. It wasn't his imagination. He was convinced that the giant retailer was putting too many consumers at risk. They had the personal information and credit card numbers of more than 25 million consumers! As he drove home that night, he decided he just couldn't let it go. But how should he handle it? Was he seeing the situation all wrong? Did Gina know things about the environment that he didn't? Was Sofia right that he was exaggerating the level of risk? They both had more experience than he did. But, after all, Ron had taken a job in cybersecurity to protect people.

He thought of his friend from college who wrote for a national tech news organization and sat down at his computer. He typed up an anonymous email detailing the shoddy audit, the potential breach risk, and management's subsequent decision to shrug their shoulders and put so many consumers at risk. He saved the email as a draft on his personal laptop. He then typed up an email to his CIO, Brandon (Gina's boss), and attached his analytics report of the potential risk. He detailed why the company had to reconsider the audit and commit resources to fixing these vulnerabilities. He sat back for a minute after editing that email and saved it as a draft. Finally, he wrote an email to the director of the audit team, Jalen, attached his analysis, and then detailed what he felt they had missed during the audit. He saved the email as a draft. After Ron had finished the three email drafts, he closed his computer. He would get a good night's sleep, eat breakfast, and then decide which emails to send in the morning.

Critical Application Questions

What direction should Ron take in the morning with his assessment of the audit? Which one is the most ethical?

How can you apply the lessons of this chapter to Ron's dilemma?

Have you been in a situation like this before? What is Ron's responsibility to his CISO? What is his responsibility to the company's customers?

What do you think of the CIO's handling of the objection about the audit?

Is it ever ethical to be a whistleblower? Are there other ethical concerns to consider in this situation?

If you were the CISO, Gina, how would you handle Ron and his report? How would you respond if Ron sent any of the three emails?

Have you been involved in a situation like this? Have you seen a passing audit that you disagreed with? How did you handle it?

What do you think of Sofia's objection that they are a retail company rather than a security company? Is she right that they are overemphasizing the vulnerabilities the audit missed?

How do you check yourself and your work when up against opposition?

CHAPTER

7

Practicing Cyber Kung Fu

"I will endeavor to exercise patience, wisdom, and self-control in all situations."
> – The Cybersecurity Code of Honor

"Patience is the road to wisdom."
> – Kao Kalia Yang, author, public speaker, and teacher

"You have power over your mind, not outside events. Realize this, and you will find strength."
> – Marcus Aurelius, Roman emperor

Jared paced slowly with his coffee in hand until he stood at the corner of his long stand-up desk. He looked through the glass window to see Jill, his CISO, on the phone a few workstations away. Jared was a lead security analyst for the fastest-growing crowd-funding start-up on the planet. He looked back to his screen to slowly reread one more time the email forwarded to him and assess its legitimacy. He had handled enough cyber incidents in his time to recognize this was not a prank. Luka, the company's new system admin, came running from the corner office in a panic. "Did you see our About page?" he yelled to Jared and anyone who would listen. Jared took a slow, deep breath, "I am looking at the attacker's communication right now." Raise-a-Fund's About page had also been transformed from a colorful and inviting informational landing spot into a concerning black screen with the picture of an angry red troll holding up one prominent finger in a defiantly obscene gesture. Their attackers also sent along an email providing evidence that they had possession of 22 million consumer credit card numbers. All signs were pointing toward a disastrous situation.

Members of IT and the security team were leaving their workstations and moving toward the CISO's office. Jill's staff had been recruited from various industries but had been together only a short time since the company was just a year old. In a few minutes, they were all gathered around the stand-up conference table for an emergency response meeting. Jill allowed her senior analyst Jared to explain that the attackers were giving them 48 hours to pay the ransom or they would release the millions of credit card numbers and identities to the dark web. They had also promised to take full control of the company's website—and had already demonstrated they had the ability to do that with their stunt on the company's About page. One of their specific demands in the note was that law enforcement should not be involved.

The company was so new that it did not yet have a plan in place for such an event, and this was becoming a desperate situation. The intensity was high, and the panic level was elevated. One analyst, Tony, began texting with their outsourced security firm. Their forensics team was already at work, and an early hypothesis suggested that the attackers were able to get in through a third-party accounting vendor, but the forensics team wouldn't be able to confirm that for several hours. The attacker group had been identified as a team from Europe who had notoriously hit several large start-up organizations in the past six months. Jill knew the group was a legitimate threat. The attackers had warned that any interference would result in the consumer data being released and the entire site being taken down.

The founder and president of Raise-a-Fund, a start-up mogul and web expert, needed to be informed along with the company's legal team. Jill wanted to gather all the necessary facts before she headed into the emergency executive team meeting. The entire situation seemed to be spinning out of control, and she knew dealing in facts was paramount. The team hadn't practiced handling a breach and had only cursory discussions of what they would do, so Jill had no idea how their billionaire president would respond to the extortionists' demands. Would they pay? Would they want to contact law enforcement immediately? There were so many unknowns.

She gathered everything they knew into one tip sheet so she would be well-informed for her meeting with the founder. As she pulled her own team together to assemble the tip sheet, there was a breathless energy in the room. She knew that everyone must work quickly, but she looked to her team, speaking in a very calm, confident tone. "Let's all take a deep breath and make sure we are thinking our way clearly through this," she paused and smiled reassuringly at her team again, saying, "It will be OK." She was intent on trying to project a sense of calm and confidence to her team. The security team hustled back to their workstations, each with specific marching orders, and Jill returned to her workspace. She sat down and took a moment to gather her thoughts. She knew from her experience the best thing she could do would be to move forward with a calm, cool, and collected attitude about this crisis. She needed good "kung fu" now more than ever.

This scene may be unfamiliar to a young practitioner, but seasoned cybersecurity professionals will understand how quickly a day can go from enjoying a latté and observing the fall leaves turn red and gold outside the office window to being in the middle of a full-blown crisis. The nature of the cybersecurity business brings with it high-pressure and high-stakes situations that arrive without warning. This is the natural landscape of cybersecurity life. Things can go wrong, and when they do, they usually go wrong quickly. There is no such thing as being 100% secure in a world with highly skilled, clever, and surprisingly malicious cyberattackers lurking in every corner across the globe.

For the cyber professional, dealing with instability and even chaos can be part of your day-to-day work. Stress can come in waves, and it can present on several fronts. First, we face the ever-present realities of the cyber arms race. When it comes to cybercriminals, it is often "us against them," and our defensive measures will always be breathlessly sprinting to keep up with the strategies of our determined adversaries. This introduces all kinds of tensions, and it also places pressure on our day-to-day decision-making.

We also have to walk in the constant tension of protecting our business, clients, and shareholders while at the same time not getting in the way of the business, clients, or shareholders. For example, that new app may need to roll out on the launch date given all the work done by the marketing team, even as you are still developing its security as the launch looms. Or that new point-of-sale system may not be 100% protected when it has to ship to meet contractual requirements. Cybersecurity is the revenue-driving mission of very few organizations. In fact, cybersecurity is usually a cost center or the price of doing business. As one chief information officer (CIO) in the medical community reminded his staff, "Our mission is to provide great healthcare, not to provide cybersecurity." Of course, we in the industry know that you can't truly provide great healthcare without providing cybersecurity to patients and their data. But that's not a distinction that most of our organizations internalize or even understand.

Ultimately, most of us in the industry must operate in the tension of how to provide the best service while keeping our organization, clients, and consumers safe and secure. These forces at work in our industry are constantly pulling at us and can place us at the center of the storm at a moment's notice. We must have the fortitude to manage this type of work.

Essential to Success: Patience, Wisdom, and Self-Control

We suggest that you cannot operate successfully in the natural tensions presented in cybersecurity without a well-developed sense of patience, wisdom, and self-control. We say *developed* because, like other ethical practices, these are essential skills that can (and need to) be learned and strengthened.

Although we think of kung fu primarily as a martial art in the West, the meaning is actually broader. In China, kung fu is rooted in the idea of study, learning, or practice that requires patience, energy, and time to complete. In its original meaning, kung fu can refer to any discipline or skill achieved through hard work and practice. This type of discipline captures a need for cyber professionals, particularly in the area of ethics.

Without developing these skills, we cannot effectively handle the pressures of cybersecurity work. Good decisions are not possible when we operate in a state of anxiety or panic. If you are new to cybersecurity, you will find it impossible to manage the fast-paced, high-pressure, critical-stakes situations that are common to your work without these qualities. They are key to your professional success and, perhaps, the success of your organization. We can exercise these critical attributes with consistent application of principles and practices. Our hope in this chapter is to provide some practical ways to develop and exercise these attributes.

We think the most reliable way to put these qualities into action is through having, knowing, and executing a well-thought-out and rehearsed plan. History provides the best illustration and lessons that can be learned, especially when considering the tragic story of the "unsinkable" passenger liner *Titanic*.

Remember the *Titanic*

In April 1912, the luxury ocean liner considered unsinkable struck an iceberg in the North Atlantic Ocean while on its way to the United States. As the ship went down, more than 1,500 passengers went with it; only 700 people survived. Later, it was discovered that there wasn't any type of emergency response plan in place for such a crisis. In fact, there weren't even enough lifeboats on board to carry all of the passengers. In the middle of trying to load the women and children on the handful of lifeboats, the crew made quite a few mistakes. Nearly all of the lifeboats were launched into the water only half-full during the absolute panic of the ship going down because the crew felt that fully loaded lifeboats would be far too heavy to be lowered into the water.[13]

One of the stunning realities of the *Titanic* disaster was that no emergency drills were carried out on board before or during that voyage. The plans were not rehearsed. In fact, the ship's captain, John Smith, canceled one scheduled lifeboat drill that was supposed to take place the morning before the *Titanic* sank. He canceled the drill because he wanted to deliver one final Sunday church service before his retirement. One wonders how many more lives may have been saved if they had just done one simple emergency drill. The sinking of the *Titanic* actually caused global outrage and led to some international nautical policy changes that still exist today. From that point on, every ship had to have enough lifeboats to evacuate every passenger. Rules and regulations were enacted to ensure that crews prepared sufficiently for this type of naval disaster.

The great irony of the *Titanic* narrative was the belief that the ship was unsinkable. Let us take note. No matter how secure we believe we are, there are icebergs nearby. Your systems may be relatively well secured, but they are *not* unhackable. You will almost certainly get hacked, and perhaps in a completely unanticipated and novel way.

Remember the *Titanic*. You need a clear and rehearsed plan for various kinds of cyberattacks, and you must consistently rehearse your incident response plan. Regularly scheduled practice helps strengthen the muscles of patience, wisdom, and self-control. As the cybersecurity landscape is in a state of constant change, it is also necessary to routinely review those emergency response policies and plans to make sure they are sufficient and up-to-date with the latest trends in attacks and defensive techniques.

A Few Principles for Emergency Planning

The familiar maxim "Failing to plan is planning to fail" is also true in cybersecurity. We must expect the unexpected. It is one of the exciting things about cybersecurity, which is generally not a boring job. We have to be on alert, stay prepared, and have a plan in place in the event of a crisis situation. Whether you are an entry-level analyst or a seasoned manager in security, it is worth considering a few principles and practices as you learn how to approach a situation with patience, wisdom, and self-control.

- **Understand the chain of command and maintain clear communication.** There should be a clear understanding of responsibilities at every level. The clearer the decision-making and communication chain of command is prior to a crisis, the more quickly and succinctly you and your team will respond.

- **Be clear about the sequence of the steps.** What if the crew of the *Titanic* had known the appropriate measures for loading people into the lifeboats to their full capacity and how to lower those boats to the water? Many of the attack scenarios in this book could have been managed more effectively if the crisis responses had been rehearsed.

- **Know your role.** Cybersecurity is a team effort. Great teams are composed of people who know their part and how to execute it. A great rock band comes together perfectly with the lead guitar, rhythm guitar, vocals, drums, and bass to create the perfect mix of sound. Every successful organization has clearly defined responsibilities: leadership, public relations, accounting, IT, cybersecurity, physical security, and more, all working to support each other. Lean into each other's strengths to find the wisdom you need in a crisis.

- **Practice makes you more perfect.** When tensions are high, and decisions need to be made at a fast pace, it is helpful to know the steps. Just like fire drills, active-shooter drills, or any high-pressure situations your organization may face, it is essential to regularly practice the execution of your response. Periodic, regular tabletop exercises (TTXs) are important in preparing for attacks. A good TTX is a carefully thought out, realistic scenario for your organization to work through and ensure everyone knows the process for handling incidents and their role in it. They also help you commit each step to memory so that when the stress is high, you can lean into the habits you have created. When emotions run high, it is critical for those ingrained habits from drills and practice to take over.

Stay Calm, Cool, and Collected

We must be able to manage our emotions in difficult situations. This is true of both leadership and frontline operators. Composure is key, and it's part of what leaders look for in the hiring process. The more composed you are, the more valuable you are in a crisis. Research shows that anger, excitement, and even sadness can affect the quality of decision-making. Anxiety in your personal life can bleed over into work decisions. Anger can lead you to make particularly high-risk choices. Emotion-based decision-making is generally not constructive and, at worst, could lead to terrible outcomes.

As leaders, there are few qualities more important than composure in the face of a difficult situation. Jill, the CISO in our opening story of this chapter, is a good model. As a leader, you are the one who sets the tone for how others will follow. Your team is watching you, and they will take their cues from you, good or bad. If you are calm, cool, and collected, your team will likely follow your example. In both of our professional roles, we try to hire leadership-level employees who have a well-developed sense of composure. As a rule, the leader's job is to solve problems, and lack of composure is generally an obstacle to effective problem-solving.

In Jonathan Haidt's important book *The Coddling of the American Mind*, he examines beliefs that are currently gripping the rising generation of students, workers, and leaders. These ideas have become increasingly embedded in the American psyche: *What doesn't kill you makes you weaker; always trust your feelings; and life is a battle between good people and evil people.* Haidt contends that these three Great Untruths and the resulting culture he calls "safetyism" has interfered with people's social, emotional, and intellectual development.

We agree that the untruth of "emotional reasoning: always trust your feelings" has gripped a large swath of the public today and that it is a terrible trend. Too many decisions are made on the basis of feelings rather than carefully deliberated, rational, objective decision-making. What you feel has some importance, but it has little cachet in good decision-making. Emotions tend not to clearly reflect the reality of a situation. As a rule, we need to set our feelings aside in order to be objective. Objectivity is central to good decisions.

If you want to stand out as a practitioner or leader, consider that many people in an active breach situation will be, internally or externally, freaking out in some way. If you can keep your composure, you will be of great value and perhaps noticed. Think about how you can remain calm and focused in a way that will differentiate you.

Here are a few tips for high-pressure situations:

- **Take deep, slow breaths.** Work to center yourself so that you can see the situation clearly. Slow, intentional breathing also oxygenates your brain and makes you more coherent.

- **Speak slowly and in measured tones.** Don't exaggerate and don't catastrophize or project into an unknown future.

- **Communicate facts; refrain from speculation.** Focus on what is known because if you follow what is known, you will be working toward a real solution.

- **Make sure you get ample rest during times of stress.** Take a break every once in a while. Go for a walk.

Call a friend. Take a nap or get a good night's sleep to clear your mind.

- **Remember to balance your work and your personal life.** Stress at work can translate to stress at home, and vice versa, unless you consciously and actively focus on separating the two.

Each time we rehearse or experience a crisis, we are training for the next one. We are building muscle memory to prepare us to respond with patience, wisdom, and self-control in the biggest moments. We would argue that these are the ingredients you need to make not just the right decisions in your daily work but also the bold and courageous decisions that can make a positive impact on the world around you.

During World War II, May 26, 1940, found a large portion of the Allied army (mostly British, French, and Belgian troops) perilously trapped by the German Army on the shores of Dunkirk in Northern France. A newly elected prime minister, who had just taken over for Neville Chamberlain, found himself in a dire crisis. Retreating from Adolf Hitler and his German army was not the start to his leadership that he wanted. Furthermore, the shallow waters off the shore of Dunkirk, the lack of ships, and the constant bombing by the German Air Force made this an impossible situation. A large portion of the Allied army could be wiped out in days. In the face of this potential catastrophe, Winston Churchill ordered the launch of "Operation Dynamo." Large ships could not get close enough to perform rescues, so small ships were needed to ferry the troops from the beaches.

The operations would begin with British Navy ships and quickly become a movement of more than 700 small ships, including privately owned small yachts and fishing boats. While Churchill lamented that retreat was not something to celebrate, the operation was a victory in the eyes of the world when 330,000 stranded soldiers were brought back safely to English shores, saving so many lives and maintaining the UK's ability to fight another day. Churchill's clear and composed leadership under such pressure, along with the incredibly calm work of evacuation by the sailors and soldiers were the catalyst for what would be known as "The Miracle of Dunkirk," and would embolden the British in their fierce resistance against the Nazis later in the war. One crisis decision made with patience, wisdom, and self-control helped change world history.

Our Job Is Not Revenge

We know there are seasoned cybersecurity professionals who are paid to go off to some island and "hack back" a group that has attacked an organization. There will be times when active cybercriminals have screwed up and exposed themselves for you and your team to consider returning the damage that they themselves have inflicted. The ethical dilemma lies in our response to that kind of opportunity. For those of us in the commercial or civilian world, it is not our job to take revenge. As security professionals, we are here to be the first line of *defense*. It isn't a good idea to act as a vigilante in cybersecurity. Taking revenge and hacking will undermine trust, which is the most valuable quality of a cyber professional. Additionally, acting as a vigilante and hacking back could get you into some serious trouble—professionally, personally, and legally. You may inadvertently hit the wrong target or cause damage to an otherwise innocent organization through whom the attacker has pivoted. Let's be careful out there!

Even penetration testing is part of a larger art of constructing defensive strategies to protect organizations from harm. For those on the periphery of cybersecurity, it is important to clarify that *hacker* isn't a bad word. It is neutral. There are good/ethical hackers and bad/unethical hackers. All of the best cyber professionals we know are great hackers. And therein lies the essence of the ethical situation: we can use our skills for good or ill. Therefore, we must commit to using our professional abilities and resources for good and for defense only, including our offensive hacking skills. When we turn our attention to attacking an attacker and shooting back, we blur the lines of who we are committed to be as professionals. In striking back in vengeance, you may accidentally inflict harm on innocent third parties.

Imagine that you are a nighttime security guard at a large retail store. Your primary job is to protect the store from loss related to shoplifting and to protect the consumers in that store. The ethic of "never stealing" is essential to the trust built in this area of work. So, what if you follow some thieves home who have stolen from your store and break into their car to steal back from them? Of course, once you, a professional committed to stopping theft, are seen breaking into someone else's property, your credibility as the person standing between your company and property loss will come into question.

No matter how long you have worked in cybersecurity and what level of leadership you are in, never give your superiors or clients any reason to doubt your integrity. If you operate in a commercial or civilian government role, resist the temptation to go on the offense against would-be attackers. Leave that to law enforcement or the military.

Develop Your Cyber Kung Fu

The cybersecurity world provides a high-stress, fast-paced, exciting line of work. Part of the fun is the adrenaline, excitement, and satisfaction that comes from saving the day in those hair-on-fire moments. The times we really get to show off our skills are when we move from being a company cost center to being a company rescue team. Your patience, wisdom, and self-control are at the heart of success and may even help define your career.

Code-Critical Application

Read the following case study and answer the questions applying what you have learned in this chapter.

Case Study: An Open Door: Vigilante Justice

Lisa and Noel are the senior officers in a technology company just outside of Austin, Texas. Lisa is the CIO of the organization, while Noel is the CISO, and they are peers in the organizational structure. The company designs systems for manufacturing groups around the world. Lisa's team has eight IT professionals, and Noel's team has three cybersecurity practitioners. Both Lisa and Noel answer directly to the president of their organization, Steve. On Tuesday, as they are finishing their sandwiches, Lisa's team discovers an active attacker in their environment and informs Noel. Noel immediately brings in Antoinette, the forensic specialist on his team, and they quite quickly determine the attack is originating from South America.

As Lisa and Noel meet with their staff and begin to go through their incident response procedures, they are immediately fascinated to learn the attacker is using a tool that has a significant security hole in it—remote code execution—so they could take control of the attacker's machine. Noel is a talented security specialist and was one of the world's most sought-after penetration testers when she ran her own consulting company. She has the expertise and the hacking chops to use the attackers' vulnerability against them. They call Steve, the company president, to apprise him of the scope of the situation.

During the call, Noel floats the idea that because they have traced the attack and understand the clear vulnerability in the tool the adversary is using, they may have an incredible advantage. She proposes that they create a document for the attacker to steal. When that document is opened, it will exploit a bug in the attacker's toolset to gain code execution on the attacker's machine. It will then search for all of the data that has been stolen and delete it. Steve is open to this proposal but wants to know the level of risk they may assume with this type of unorthodox response to the attack. Lisa objects to Noel's proposed response, pointing out that they already have clear policies and procedures in place that they must follow. She wants to contact the authorities and go through the steps that they have rehearsed for the past year. Noel argues her case that not only do they have the ability to delete what has been stolen, but they have the right to do so before the attackers use that data or abuse their customers. In fact, Noel notes, perhaps they have an ethical obligation to do so to protect their customers using every reasonable and available option. Also, Noel points out that they could hack back and disable the attackers' systems rendering them unable to do anyone else any harm, thus preventing damage to future victims.

Steve is fascinated with Noel's approach to this current crisis. It is an aggressive countermeasure to prevent the attackers from having any impact on their business, and it also protects the company and, even more importantly, its customers. He tells Lisa and Noel that he needs a few minutes to consider this course of action but sees how it could be the most beneficial response. Lisa objects again and points out that most attacks are pivoted through a series of other systems. She is concerned about the impact, legal and otherwise, as well as the possibility of damaging other system owners through the process of Noel's unorthodox response. When their document's hidden code deletes their own data pilfered by the attacker, who's to say that it won't delete other data, perhaps sensitive data of an innocent person?

She also has concerns about the limited amount of information they have about the hacking group. For instance, what if the group is financed by a foreign country? What if the information they are stealing has implications they know nothing about? Furthermore, as they gather information on the data that has been compromised, are they seeing the full picture of the breach this quickly? The president ends the conference call and tells Lisa and Noel he will make his decision on a course of action at the top of the hour after he consults the company's attorney. The two head back to their teams to plan the next steps in response to this attack.

Critical Application Questions

What direction do you believe the president should take?

Is it ethical to hack back if they are sure they can delete the stolen data?

What do you think of Noel's objection about other entities that could be affected by Lisa's plan?

What are some other considerations that Noel and Lisa did not present to Steve about the situation?

What are some objections you would make to Lisa's strategy? What do you think of them abandoning the incident handling plans they have in place for this particular situation? Have you been involved in a situation like this? How did you handle it?

8

No Sticky Fingers Allowed

"I will not steal and will do everything within my power to prevent theft in all its forms."

– The Cybersecurity Code of Honor

"A thief is a thief, whether he steals a diamond or a cucumber."

– Unknown Author

"The accomplice is as bad as the thief."

– Unknown Author

James is a young, bright, rising cybersecurity professional who writes programs for detecting attacks at his regional utility company called Energy Inc. in the midwestern United States. Just four years out of university, he recently accepted a job offer from a large New York City firm and submitted his two weeks' notice to his current employer. He will be taking a significant pay raise and moving up the org chart in this big-city position. James has been busy the last few days briefing his team and his supervisor on his daily responsibilities. Fortunately, they are filling his role with another member of his current team, so he is able to help that person understand the scope of his work before his final day at the company. It will make the transition easier for the security team at Energy Inc. James is well-liked by his team and supervisor, and his track record is pristine. His chief information security officer (CISO), Dawn, did all she could to retain James but understands the allure of the New York City job. It is Tuesday of James' final week, and the team is already planning a going-away happy-hour celebration on Friday to send James off on his new adventure.

James has started the usual process everyone undergoes as they prepare to leave one job for another. Each evening, he tosses several personal items from his workspace into his backpack to carry back to his apartment. By Friday, his family pictures, collectibles, coffee mugs, awards, movie posters, and professional certifications will make the trek home, but these aren't the only items that James has decided to take with him into his next position.

Last year, James wrote a unique intrusion detection program for Energy Inc. that became wildly effective in identifying a specific series of attack types. He casually thought that because he authored the program, it is obvious that he has the right to take it with him to his next job. Without asking anyone at the company or even giving it a second thought, James uploaded the code to a cloud-based repository, just like he had tossed his personal stuff into his backpack. It never occurred to James that there was an ethical dilemma involved in this decision. After all, he wrote the program so he could take a copy of it and use it elsewhere, right?

James thinks the security program can be repurposed and effectively applied to other industries, particularly for his new employer. It could be a big early win to introduce a version of it to the security team at his new job. And then, who knows. . .maybe he'll open source it to help the whole cybersecurity community! James thought, "It's all about making the world a better place, you know!"

The CISO, Dawn, is closing down her day on Thursday and has actually just answered an email about her star employee, James, and the plan to celebrate his final day when she receives a notification of potentially suspicious activity from one of her other security team members. The security team noticed an unusual file transfer to a cloud storage system—something triggered a signature-based intrusion detection system on their network. As Dawn reviews the email, she realizes that this upload has come from James' workstation. A brief look at the upload shows that the package included a series of strings for various attack tools, which triggered the detection. But those strings were actually part of the company's detection program that James built. Dawn shakes her head in disbelief. She looks at the clock and realizes that James is probably still in the office, but this conversation is not going to be a casual one.

Although James wrote the program, he did so on company time on company hardware for the express purpose of defending the company network and systems. In Dawn's mind, this is a clear violation of ethics. She picks up the phone to call Brent, the vice president of human resources, to discuss the situation and how she should handle it. The conversation with Brent prompts her next call to the company's internal legal counsel.

In the next few hours, right as he is about to finish his last day of work, James will go from being celebrated to facing a lawsuit from his current employer. In a process that will draw out over two years of litigation, James will also lose his job at the New York City firm before he even has a chance to begin his first day. Although Energy Inc. ultimately decides to drop the charges, James' career as a security professional is tarnished. His story represents a common dilemma in today's cyber work culture. His rationale to take the program because "he wrote it" (and ignore the reality that it is the intellectual property of his current employer) presents a perfect example of the hyper-importance of maintaining clear boundaries about property in our industry. We must avoid even the appearance of having sticky fingers in the world of cybersecurity. But this isn't just a problem among cyber professionals, this is a greater cultural issue.

If It's Free, It's for Me?

Those of you of a certain age will remember the arrival of the music file-sharing Napster application in the 1990s as the world transitioned from records, cassettes, and CDs into the era of digital music. Napster brought lawsuits, protests, and a new dilemma for how to protect the property of recording artists. How would copyright laws be applied, and how might recording artists and record companies capitalize on music if it was being taken for free on the Internet? Of course, that quickly evolved into the question of digitally pirating movies, which became a prominent trend in the early 2000s. People with any computer proficiency at all were downloading all types of "free" media. Of course, technology moves more quickly than our ethical approaches to new dilemmas that accompany the wonderful advancements made. The sad reality is that our ethics always seem to lag behind.

If this conversation doesn't have you thinking about Julian Assange, then you probably aren't working directly in the security industry. His story is a lightning rod in our line of work. For the uninitiated, Assange ran the Wikileaks organization, which focused on publicly sharing leaked information from government agencies and corporations that exposed corruption and other malfeasance. He is seen by some in the cyber community as a hero and by others as a villain. The theme that runs through the Assange conversation has risen to an almost religious belief among some in the hacking community that information "wants to be free."

If you really study what is happening across the world with digital property, information, and intellectual property, you will find that we are still in a Wild Wild West era where nearly everything can be stolen, and too often, it is. Now more than ever, we need a concerted effort and commitment to ethical decision-making when it comes to intellectual property.

It is true that in some other cultures, what we in Western culture consider stealing is instead considered good business. For instance, if you walk by a hotel with a familiar brand name on the marquee in some countries, you may go to check in only to be stunned to find that the hotel has no associations with the international brand on the outside marquee. There is a joke among some in the cybersecurity industry that if you lose information in a crash and don't have a backup, you shouldn't worry too much because someone in China probably snagged a copy of your data while hacking you and has a backup that you can buy.

The idea that "if it is free, it's for me" is too often the guiding ethic. Sadly, not only is this approach illegal, it has huge economic and ethical implications. From an economic perspective, while making a surreptitious copy of information doesn't deprive its original owner of still having that data, it does prevent the owner from having *exclusive* access and use of the information. That limits the owner of economic value and, if such practices are widespread, might lower the value of information and the investment people are willing to make in its creation. From an ethical perspective, that copied information may contain sensitive personal or business secrets, which could be devastating if disclosed.

Avoid a "Robin Hood" Narrative

The challenge, of course, is that we work in an industry where many of us are trained to do our jobs by learning to "break in" to target computer systems to identify vulnerabilities and ascertain their risk. Our industry has many practitioners who are trained with offensive skills, and yet our job is to defend and protect property. As such, it is essential that we embrace a clearly defined ethic of not taking what is not ours.

Here is the reality: just because making a copy of a file that doesn't belong to you doesn't *feel* like stealing your neighbor's car doesn't mean it isn't stealing. Theft is theft. Remember, the currency of our work comes down to trust. We operate in the trust business. We come to work to stop others from stealing what does not belong to them.

Many in the cybersecurity industry were enticed to do this work because someone needed to help stop the bad attackers' open season on whomever they wanted to steal from, whenever they wanted to steal. *Preventing theft is the essence of our work*. It is the goal of our job at every level. In a profession dedicated to serving and protecting others, it is fundamental that we commit to a clear and undisputed principle: do *not* steal.

We must affirm intellectual property is property. In our era of hacking evolution, the lines are too often blurred between good and bad. The demarcation between what is theft and what isn't often "feels" indistinct when we work in a cyber culture with some people focused on "Robin Hood" stories. Of course, Robin Hood is the English mythological character who would rob from the rich to provide and care for the poor. Stealing. . .but for a good cause. It sounds ethically acceptable, right? When we begin to decide when and where theft is good or bad, it creates all kinds of ethical challenges. Who's to say we aren't all Robin Hood in one way or another? Who determines that stealing a program and releasing it publicly for free isn't for the greater good? Just consider that once we justify our behaviors, believing we can take what is not ours in Robin Hood–style, we have a major problem. This cavalier attitude toward the property of others invites disaster. It is best to avoid any appearance of being a Robin Hood.

A Tragedy of "Free Information"

One of the more controversial and high-profile cases of information appropriation this century ended in incredible, utter tragedy. If you aren't familiar with the Aaron Swartz story, he was one of the brightest young programming minds, entrepreneurs, and hacktivists in the mid-2000s. He was involved in the development of RSS and even given the title cofounder of Reddit. In 2011, Swartz was arrested after he connected a computer in a closet to a Massachusetts Institute of Technology (MIT) network and set it to download thousands of academic articles from a guest user account issued to him by the university. His supposed intent was to release those articles to the world for free. Of course, Swartz had no prior record, and his intentions in doing this weren't something you would normally classify as criminal. By all accounts, he was a great young man.

But federal prosecutors charged him with two counts of wire fraud and eleven violations of computer fraud that carried a maximum penalty of $1 million in fines, 35 years in prison, asset forfeiture, and restitution to be paid to MIT.

Swartz and his attorneys declined an option to plea bargain with federal prosecutors who were offering him six months in a minimum-security prison. Two days after those prosecutors rejected a counteroffer sent from the Swartz legal defense team, he was found dead by suicide in his Brooklyn apartment. It was an absolute heartbreaking tragedy.

Swartz has since been inducted into the Internet Hall of Fame, and as time passes, he is increasingly celebrated. It is important to note that while we aren't weighing in on what happened in the prosecution of Swartz, we are pointing to the perils of operating without careful attention to and vigilance about intellectual property rights. No matter the intent, it is heartbreaking to think that Swartz's life ended because of such a situation. We hope it is at least a cautionary tale about the idea of playing Robin Hood in the cyber world. There were simply no winners in this truly devastating situation.

Intellectual Property Is Property

The clear line to stand on is this: intellectual property *is* property. There is no room for this to be a gray area. We need to avoid all appearances of impropriety. We are to protect intellectual property and never, under any circumstances, are we to participate in theft. Hearkening back to the previous chapter, we shouldn't engage in it even if we are "stealing property back." A friendly reminder: trust is central to our work. You *have* to demonstrate that you are responsible with the keys that unlock sensitive information. It is always helpful to be reflective and thoughtful about your decisions. Understand your ethical boundaries *before* you are put in critical situations. "Do not steal" is as simple and straightforward an ethic as you can practice. You will not steal code, you will not steal data, you will not steal music or games, you will not steal streaming services, and you will not steal that personal dinner with the company credit card. And that applies even if you *think* there is no way for you to get caught. In a world full of confusing moral dilemmas, this is decidedly *not* one of them.

In an effort to avoid gray lines, it is important to be faithful with our access. As cybersecurity professionals, we often have keys to many different types of systems for work, but that doesn't allow us to access all their data without express permission to do our jobs. Likewise, your employer has probably provided a license to all kinds of software that you need to accomplish your tasks. But typically, you aren't authorized to simply use those programs at home for other purposes outside of your employment. You may have the keys to the kingdom, but you don't *own* the kingdom.

A CISO told us the story of one of his employees, whom we'll call Mark. Mark was a great employee for the company but was also running a side business as a freelancer developing software. As his freelance business grew, so did his reputation in the business community. One day, the CISO was at a local cybersecurity luncheon talking with the owner of a prominent local start-up that he had just gotten to know. This owner happened to mention how great Mark's "development work" had been for his own small company. The CISO was unaware that Mark was doing development as a side business but became quite concerned when he realized that Mark was using a copyrighted software development environment licensed by the company to run his own side projects without obtaining permission. It led to a pretty serious conversation and, eventually, Mark's resignation. The CISO told us that Mark had earned quite a bit of money utilizing tools that were not his to do work that had nothing to do with the company.

Stealing can be a slippery slope. If you are using company-licensed software at home, it should be for the expressed purpose of your job. Company software for company work. Another of our acquaintances who works on the accounting side of the C-suite tells the story of having to terminate one of her best managers at one point for abusing the office supplies policy. The senior accountant was using the office supplies budget to buy things to furnish his home. He was also taking a significant amount of office supplies to use for his spouse's small business. The issue began with this manager taking reams of paper and pens from the supply closet. The problem slowly escalated over time until he was ordering office furniture to take home, all paid for by the company budget. The stealing became so consistent that his executive assistant eventually reported the abuse.

Research shows that with the COVID-19 pandemic came a huge increase in the abuse of company credit cards. There are plenty of articles highlighting this trend and discussing how to prevent employee theft.[14] "Credit card fraud is one of the most common abuses committed by employees. American corporations lose approximately $50B and 1.8% in revenue annually because of employee theft.

For many companies, employee credit card misuse usually begins with small charges, goes unnoticed for years, and adds up over time." There are some pretty significant and alarming statistics about all kinds of employee theft that we think are important to talk about, namely, the admission that 75% of employees surveyed admit to stealing something from their company at least once. And 37.5%, nearly 4 out of every 10 people, admit to stealing from their employer at least twice.[15] Because cybersecurity work is predicated on preventing theft, we need to be extra vigilant in how we treat property that does not belong to us.

To Catch a Thief, We Must Train Like One

It is our duty to prevent theft, yet one of the great challenges in cybersecurity is that to stop a thief many have to learn how to think like a thief. Cybersecurity professionals are trained to understand thievery. Because many of us have been trained in the offensive arts, such as penetration testing and red teaming, we have the ability and tools to be thieves. Yet, with great power comes great responsibility. Our expertise in understanding thievery is exactly why we should never blur the lines and why it is so easy to.

Choices Have Consequences

Could you make more money as a cybersecurity professional using the hacking skills you have learned to commit theft? Perhaps. Would you end up wearing an orange jumpsuit and spending a portion of your life in a cell? Perhaps. Even small choices to steal are important in the big picture. With every action we take, we are always deciding who we are going to be. Research tells us that theft generally begins with the small things. It is best to never take that first step.

Let's touch on the larger ethical picture, even though it may be obvious to most. Virtually every major ethical framework or religious teaching in the world adheres to some form of clear prohibition against stealing. With the exception of some rare philosophical constructs, there is virtually no moral code in human history that doesn't explicitly articulate that theft is wrong. Yes, one can hold up examples of stealing food to avoid starvation or stealing a terrorist's bomb to save the lives of its intended victims, but "Robin Hood examples" such as these are potential exceptions, not the basis of an ethical framework. The canon of law in Western civilization has codified the illegality of theft for more than 2,000 years. The handful of cultures where stealing is acceptable or normative are generally places where corruption or totalitarianism is the norm.

It is also helpful to be reminded that the line of demarcation between good folks and bad folks in cybersecurity is rooted in the utter simplicity of whether or not one steals information and/or the property of others. Theft is the foundational defining action of bad actors in cybersecurity. For those of us who work in cybersecurity, we choose every minute of every day. The smallest choices to take what is not ours opens the door to the more significant forms of threat.

There is a mythological story about theft told by the Blackfoot Native American tribe chronicled by the University of Oklahoma.[16] In the tale, an old man comes to stay with the sun. When they both become hungry, the sun suggests that they go out deer hunting together. The sun wears a special pair of leggings to set fire to the brush and drive the deer out into the open where they can capture it easily. As their day winds down, the old man determines that he will steal the sun's leggings and use them to hunt deer more easily. While the sun is asleep, he steals the leggings and runs away, only to wake up and find himself back in the sun's home. When the sun questions him about why he is asleep with the leggings, he tells the sun that he decided to use them as a pillow. The next evening, the old man tries to steal the leggings again, only to wake up and find himself back in the sun's lodge. In the myth, the old man realizes that the whole world is the sun's lodge. Thus, no matter where he runs with the leggings to hide, he will be found out. The Native American parable points out the universal truth that we cannot run away from our immoral choices. There is truth in this ancient tale. While few who steal may be caught the first time, research shows that with thefts like shoplifting, most who commit theft will continue it over and over and over until they get caught. Eventually, what you take from others will come out in the light of day.

All I Really Need to Know I Learned in Kindergarten

Our friend recently walked into his young daughter's kindergarten classroom and noticed a list of rules posted by the teacher that included "No Sticky Fingers" with the subtitle "Don't take what isn't yours." These basic lessons are, of course, essential to the function of a healthy community and culture. It struck him how much pain and suffering could be avoided if we could simply adhere to those types of grade-school moral teachings. Our friend's experience harkens back to Robert Fulghum's famous book *All I Really Need to Know I Learned in Kindergarten*, where Fulghum reminds his adult readers of a simple code for getting along with others. Number six on Fulghum's list: "Don't take things that aren't yours."

We've presented you with the temptations and challenges of property rights in cybersecurity, yet the wisdom of a kindergarten lesson still holds up as a foundational truth to our daily life. A friendly reminder: people must trust you. Your career depends on it.

Code-Critical Application

Read the following case study and answer the questions applying what you have learned in this chapter.

Case Study: Something Borrowed and Something New

Andy had completed his certification for a new area of security programming and was excited to get his hands on the newly released software that Tech-Corp had recently adopted. He and his team were in charge of designing new software to protect against the ever-present reality of attackers trying to break in and steal files from the technology engineering company. Andy was well compensated and enjoyed his job. He was gaining a reputation as a reliable and bright contributor to the security division at his company.

One day over lunch, Andy and one of his co-workers in the security division, Victoria, were approached by an engineer who worked for Tech-Corp in the medical design division. He explained to them he was doing some of his own software dev work outside of the scope of his current job for a large retail company on the West Coast. The engineer's name was Mehdy, and he wanted to hire Andy and Victoria to help on his side project. They were resistant until he told them how much the company was paying for his work. If they could help him, he would pay them both 15% of the total fee.

They walked back from lunch that day having agreed to some work on Mehdy's project after hours. Victoria was going to use the extra money for a vacation, and Andy had been saving up for a new motorcycle. Several weeks into their side project for Mehdy, Andy realized how beneficial it would be if he used the newly adopted software by his employer, Tech-Corp, to help him with some of the programming on Mehdy's work. He talked with Victoria about how they might go about licensing the software outside of work, but the cost was prohibitive. They both agreed that if they simply were conscientious about working off the company clock, it wouldn't hurt anyone.

The two finished the security programming for Mehdy's project and moved on with their lives. Andy bought a Harley Davidson with the extra check, and Victoria planned a backpacking trip to Spain. Several weeks later, they noticed that Mehdy was absent from work. They didn't see him on campus, around the company cafeteria, or in the break room where they would normally hang out and play ping-pong. Victoria decided to follow up and text Mehdy to see where he had been. It wasn't unusual for engineers to travel for long periods of time at their company.

That afternoon, Victoria walked into Andy's office with a concerned look on her face. "Mehdy was let go last week," she said forebodingly. "His department manager said he violated company policy by doing freelance design work." They learned that Mehdy had also borrowed some of the company engineering software to do his freelance work for the outside retailer and as a result was now looking for a new place to work. Andy was immediately concerned, "Maybe we need to go to Leslie and talk about this?" Leslie was the chief information officer (CIO) and head of their division. She was a great leader and had been very complimentary of Victoria's and Andy's work in recent reviews. Victoria shook her head, "There is no way we are talking to her about this." The two went back and forth on the merits of confessing to their boss about engaging in an outside project. Technically, Victoria argued, there wasn't a clear policy about freelancing in the security team's employment agreements. That was something specific to the engineering employment agreement where Mehdy worked. Still, they agreed to take a day or so to think about what they should do.

Tech-Corp's CIO, Leslie, was pulled into a meeting with the vice president of engineering and the head of human resources that same day. They sat Leslie down to explain their concern that two of her security team specialists utilized company software to assist an engineer who had just been terminated with outside work. Myles, the vice president of engineering, explained the company's clear policy forbidding engineers from doing freelance or retainer work for other entities. The human resources (HR) specialist, Cindy, pointed out that the cybersecurity employees hadn't signed any similar clauses in their agreements. So, were Andy and Victoria's actions using company software to work on outside security programming worthy of termination?

The three executives met for the next hour trying to decide how to proceed. Leslie was adamant that her employees had great records and that this was the first instance of anything that merited discipline. The vice president of engineering felt that misusing software was theft and that they should be terminated. Furthermore, some log analysis showed that they had actually worked on developing Mehdy's program on company computers but after company hours.

The case would be presented to the CIO the next day. Leslie felt unsure that her boss would side with her view. She told the human resources specialist that she needed the evening to think through how she would proceed. After all, these were both talented employees. The coming days would determine if Andy and Victoria's choice to borrow (or steal) company resources would leave them looking for new employment.

Critical Application Questions

Considering some of the scenarios we have discussed throughout the book, how would you proceed if you were Leslie?

Can you identify with Andy and Victoria in this scenario? If they haven't violated company policy about freelance work, then have they done anything wrong?

Does using company software in this instance constitute theft in your mind? Why or why not?

If you are Andy and Victoria, how can you move forward in a way that may restore trust with their managers and stakeholders?

Have you been involved in a situation like this at work before? Describe and discuss what happened.

What are some challenges to consider in this situation?

9

It's None of Your Business

"I will protect and respect the privacy of others."
> – The Cybersecurity Code of Honor

"Privacy is an inherent human right, and a requirement
for maintaining the human condition with dignity
and respect."
> – Bruce Schneier, cryptographer and author

"It's none of your damn business."
> – Evelyn Hiddings, Ed's nana

Dwight is the system administrator at a local state
university. Angela is a professor in the computer science department who has taught at the university for more
than a decade. The two met at a faculty luncheon and hit it
off. They dated for several months before Angela broke off

their relationship, and Dwight has taken this new reality a little contentiously. Dwight is a valued employee at the university. He shows up on time and is always helpful with the staff, which includes a number of older professors who often struggle to integrate technology into their classrooms. The administration loves Dwight's dedication to supporting the staff, and he enjoys being on campus and interacting with the educators.

Last week, as Dwight was leaving the administration building, he noticed Angela walking into the cafeteria with an English professor named Robert. Of course, it bothered him a little bit. He wasn't quite over the breakup. He was on his way to the president's office for a meeting about a new tech initiative on campus that would require him to lead a training session. Later that day, he happened to notice Robert and Angela walking across campus together again. Unbeknown to him, the two were working on a departmental collaboration that was part of a state-wide educational initiative. Dwight returned to his office with hurt feelings. When Angela broke up with him, she never mentioned dating anyone else. He sat down at his desk and began to work through his long to-do list. But as the day began to wind down, his mind wandered back to Angela, and curiosity simply got the best of him.

In his day-to-day job, he has admin access to the email server used by Angela's department and decided to look at her email, simply to browse the subject lines and senders. He justified it to himself that it was no more personal than reading a postcard. But as he browsed, he noticed an email from Robert with the subject line "Meeting tonight." Overcome with curiosity, Dwight opened the email that detailed Robert and Angela's plans to meet for dinner.

Several days later, Dwight and Angela found themselves standing in line together before a meeting in the administration building. After some small talk, Dwight, forgetting where he had learned about it, casually mentioned her dinner with Robert. The conversation quickly became uncomfortable, and they went their separate ways. When Angela finally returned to her office that day, she sat down at her desk and began to review her sent emails. She wondered whether Dwight might have violated her privacy. She knew Dwight's role as system administrator would provide him with that kind of access but never dreamed he would abuse it. Dwight had always been very earnest and above reproach with the access and privileges that came with his job, but she had a hunch that he had read her email.

She changed her password and then decided to walk over to human resources and file a complaint. She sat down with Sally, the human resources director, and explained the entire situation. Sally agreed that they would look into the logs to see if Dwight had abused his administrative privileges. Over the next few weeks, Dwight would face some pretty serious consequences for invading the privacy of his co-worker.

Now, you are probably reading Dwight's story and thinking, "I'd never do something like that!" But the reality is that small invasions of privacy are a constant issue in the greater tech industry (not just cybersecurity). And it takes only one impulsive decision to violate someone else's right to privacy. Not long ago, Meta, who already has a long history of publicly reported privacy concerns, released a statement about disciplining a large group of employees for illegally accessing user accounts. If you work in tech, you are already aware that privacy is a huge challenge. For security professionals in particular, it raises the following question: *with unlimited access to so much private information, how do you properly maintain a commitment to protect and respect the privacy of others?*

In case you are wondering why this final chapter in *The Code of Honor* is about privacy, let us remind you that the innovations of our age have brought a near-continuous digital trail of our thoughts, health, wealth, and personal lives. The places we go on our phones and keyboards often reflect the life that we choose not to share with others. Our conversations that went unrecorded and unnoticed two decades ago are now texted or emailed with clear and persistent records available to the wrong eyes. We have digital evidence of arguments between spouses and serious conversations about the lives of our children over email and text. We make financial and medical decisions online; we even do therapy on the Web now. Your search engine history dutifully records your fleeting thoughts and inquiries about all manner of hopes, fears, delights, and more. All of the things that may have constituted our "private life" years ago are now online (and on record somewhere). Just because they are now discoverable doesn't mean that they shouldn't be protected.

Curiosity Can Kill the Cat

Every human being has an inherent right to privacy. This is long-established and globally accepted as a human right. The Universal Declaration of Human Rights is considered by generations of governments and leaders around the globe as an authoritative standard of human rights. It was established by the United Nations in 1948, and declares the following in Article 12: "No one shall be subjected to arbitrary interference with his privacy, family, home or correspondence, nor to attacks upon his honour and reputation. Everyone has the right to the protection of the law against such interference or attacks."

A person's privacy is deeply connected to a person's inherent dignity, which connects the first plank of the Cybersecurity Code of Honor with the last. One of the threads of this book is that despite the screens we work behind, we work in a human business. Our charge is to protect real human beings. Because every person has dignity and value, we therefore hold that every person has a right to privacy.

The same curiosity that makes you good at your job is the same quality that can get you into trouble. We cannot have a conversation about protecting privacy in cybersecurity without discussing personal self-control (plank #6 of the code of honor).

Cybersecurity professionals often have the keys to very personal information of our user base. Therefore, the use of those keys must be carefully considered and monitored for the sake of accountability. It means we have to look away at times, and it means we need to avoid even the appearance of violating the privacy of others. It is easy to violate someone's privacy, even by accident. We must use self-restraint because it is natural to want to go where we are not supposed to go.

Perhaps you've heard the phrase, "Curiosity killed the cat," which dates back to Shakespeare. It is a proverb used to warn of the dangers of unnecessary investigation, and it suggests that being curious can sometimes lead to danger or misfortune.

We're surrounded by examples of the forbidden having attraction. Consider early childhood development psychology experiments: just tell a small child they can play with any toy in the room *except* for the red block, and you know what will very likely happen. This issue is represented in our stories, mythologies, and movies. In JRR Tolkien's mythology, Gollum must have the One Ring at all costs, even though it disfigures, consumes, and ultimately will destroy him. In the famous *War Games* movie from the 1980s, Matthew Broderick's character David Lightman can play any computer game he wants to, but he instead uses a restricted password so that he can play Protovision's games before they are released publicly. Of course, he mistakes his access to Protovision with the computer in charge of the United States, nuclear launch codes and mayhem ensues. These examples reflect the truth that we must be on guard against our own curious nature.

The Golden Rule Applied to Cybersecurity

You've likely heard of the Golden Rule, which is meant to teach us to treat others as we want to be treated. The concept of doing to others as you'd want them to do to you is an idea represented in different phrasings throughout the world's great religions and moral codes. It is a relatively universal moral code. In cybersecurity, it could be translated into practical phrasing, such as every time you investigate someone's system, approach it with the same discretion that you'd want them to use if the roles were reversed. In the very same breath with which we pledge to protect the people we serve from theft, we must also be as vigilant about safeguarding their privacy—no matter the situation. It is important to remind ourselves that there are often only two groups of people that can access these private records—us (cybersecurity and IT professionals) and bad actors.

Our friend Preston took over a role at a regional dairy company when he was right out of college. At 24, he was hired as the system administrator and spent most of his time attending to the mundane computer issues that you might imagine would present at a dairy company in the early 2000s. His day-to-day role wasn't particularly engaging, and he recalls getting bored at work and deciding to investigate the chief executive officer's (CEO's) email. He had picked up the password one day when he was troubleshooting the CEO's desktop in the corner office at the top of the facility with the windows looking over the small town. It was a small choice to snoop around. Preston explains that he did it because he could and because he knew he shouldn't. But that small step soon escalated to snooping through other accounts to compare his salary to other co-workers and to investigate who was getting a raise. He didn't realize how much he had stepped over the line as a young employee until much later in his career, when he began working as a security professional.

His early failures and experience have made him introspective about the kind of security professional he wants to be. He was recently promoted to the chief information security officer (CISO) position at a prominent company and now lectures his team about clear privacy protections. Preston told us that he creates clearly defined protocols with specific checks and balances to help everyone keep their eyes in the right place when they are doing investigative work. But most of all, he reminds his people to treat others as they would want to be treated.

Stay in Your Lane

In cybersecurity, protecting the privacy of others is often as simple as focusing on your particular responsibility. Just because you have the keys to the entire hotel doesn't mean you can go investigate room number three when you are only supposed to be cleaning up room number two. For those of you in the C-suite who don't do ground-level security work, understand that this requires security professionals to have character and to be discerning. They must know when to look away. This is often as easy as just focusing on the actual job at hand and not deviating from an assigned task. The challenge can be as straightforward as looking the other way as we sit with people when we ask them to type in the passwords to their system.

Ed remembers several years ago sitting with some fellow cybersecurity instructors during a lunch break from teaching. We all sat around the table with our computers, eating quickly and trying to respond to any urgent email that popped up that morning while we were teaching. I tried to furtively type in my password to log into my system. One of my colleagues then blurted out my password. I looked up at him in shock. He said, "I shoulder surfed your password," he said with quite a bit of glee. Yes, I had tried unsuccessfully to hide my password. But I was stunned that my so-called friend would violate my privacy that way, not only seeing my password but announcing it publicly. I was stunned. I tried to coach my fellow instructor on his ethical lapse as I moved away to change my password quickly and furtively. To this day, I still have concerns about that shoulder-surfing interloper.

A young security professional told us that he was working on the system of a key executive in his organization. As he was sorting out a macro virus delivered through a phishing email to this executive's account, he came across a long series of emails between the executive and a recruiter. It was obvious from the subject lines that the executive was accepting a job with a competing organization, but this security professional explained to us that he simply had to keep that information confidential. Could it affect the company that he was working for? Yes. In fact, it did, with a big impact on the stock price after the change was announced publicly.

Was he supposed to see that kind of information when he was working to fix the system? It was right in front of his face. But it was also *out of the scope* of what he was supposed to do. He leaned into protecting the privacy of this particular executive and kept that information private even though he felt that he was violating his sense of loyalty to the company. From our point of view, he made the right call by staying in his lane.

Four Questions to Help Avoid Impropriety

Staying focused on the scope of your job is vital in protecting the privacy of others. We are there to safeguard, not to investigate, the personal lives of our clients, co-workers, bosses, or shareholders. Here are a few questions you can employ to keep yourself accountable.

- **First, is this information essential to what I am working to investigate or trying to accomplish?** If it isn't, you don't need to see it.

- **Second, is this information something that I would want others to see or know about if they were working on my system?** This goes back to the "treat others as you would want to be treated" lesson. We are often going to come across others' personal stuff as we work, so it is important to get in the habit of looking the other way.

- **Third, am I getting into information here that was not intended for me?** It is a simple and straightforward question. Just because you can access information doesn't give you the right to access it.

- **Finally, as you move into a security task, you need to ask: is this something that I need to be investigating alone?** Make sure you are following your organization's official policies and procedures and using the wisdom of the people around you to navigate circumstances where the lines appear to be blurred. If you see something that looks illegal, dangerous, or unethical, discreetly ask an appropriate person in your organization for their advice. You may need to reach out to human resources or your in-house legal team for support on the issue.

Remember, cybersecurity and especially decision-making about the privacy aspects of our field do not lend themselves to "lone-wolf" behavior. If you are accessing areas of sensitive information, have someone else on your team working with you. If you are going to work around sensitive financial files, have a superior with you observing. It is always best to plan ahead for these types of situations. If you are a leader, have policies and procedures in place to guide your team.

Each Time You Cross the Line, It Becomes Easier

Our friend has a big family dog named Butch that is treated like child in their home. The dog loves to escape the yard and run all through the neighborhood. The family had to buy an invisible fence to keep the dog secure on their one-acre lot. Invisible fence systems train the dog to listen for a certain frequency when nearing the line at the edge of the property. That signal warns the dog of an impending deterrent shock from the collar if he gets close enough to the line. Butch had been properly trained to respond to the collar and stop when he heard the signal. But curiously, Butch likes to run more than he minds being shocked. Over a few hours' time, Butch kept inching closer and closer to the line until he ran right through it. Sure, it was uncomfortable in the moment, but he made it out of the yard quickly and was soon able to go on his unimpeded tour of the neighborhood. His owners adjusted the settings on the fence to strengthen the shock, but this did not deter Butch. Each time he ran through the shock, the less he seemed to mind it at all. Finally, the owners capitulated, gave up the invisible fence idea, and are building a large privacy fence for their beloved Butch. We are curious to see how Butch responds.

The moral of the Butch story is that the more we get comfortable with crossing some line, the easier it is to do. It's kind of a shame we don't get shocked for violating someone's privacy the way Butch did when he crossed the property line. This is why we urge you to make decisions that are clearly above reproach routinely. Yes, doing the right thing is a habit. So, we encourage you to practice doing the right thing to protect privacy. A friendly reminder: there is a huge difference between what you *can do* and what you *should do*. Privacy is essential, so we must create good habits in our daily work practices to honor it.

We Hurt Real Human Beings

It begins with the celebrity who checks into the hospital. The hospital's on-site cybersecurity professional is just curious—why is the celebrity on the cardiology floor? There emerges the temptation to look, to get out of one's assigned lane and investigate what is going on with the celebrity. This happens again. The next time the cybersecurity professional pushes a little bit further. Eventually, a line has been crossed so often that it becomes a habit when a celebrity is admitted to the facility to go look it up. It starts with sharing private information with friends and family, and maybe that grows until the cybersecurity practitioner is sharing the information with a website or a news source. It gets a little easier each time.

If it sounds familiar, it should. Reading patient records is a violation of their privacy, but it happens all the time. Let's take just one organization as an example. In 2003, there was a case at the UCLA Medical Center where a disgruntled employee began to spy on the organization's electronic records. He logged into the system 323 times before he was caught. In 2005, a handful of UCLA Medical Center employees received disciplinary action for peeking into Brittany Spears' records after the birth of her son. In 2008, it happened again, but this time, the staff was caught reading Spears' psychiatric evaluations. After this second event, the university medical facility fired 13 employees, suspended 6 others, and took disciplinary action against 6 doctors.

You would think that this type of disciplinary action against employees who invaded the privacy of others would be a deterrent, but it was not. It happened again at UCLA during Farah Fawcett's battle with cancer.[17] And again, with Maria Shriver, a former television news personality and ex-wife of the action movie star and former California Governor Arnold Schwarzenegger. We aren't suggesting that there is something wrong with the UCLA health organization; we are pointing out that the problem is so rampant that it can recur in one group repeatedly despite the measures put in place. The names may be familiar, but it is important to note that these violations hurt real human beings. Imagine if one of these people was part of your immediate family.

You may be familiar with the long list of whistleblowers and admissions from the Meta/Facebook organization.[18] Over the years, Facebook has commercialized quite a bit of information, monetizing the information users share with the organization.[19] When third-party apps began to enter the platform, it is public record that Facebook falsely claimed that the apps could access only the data they needed to function properly. We know those apps could access each user's personal data, and even users who had never authenticated the applications could have their private information collected.[20] Many prominent social media platforms have been outed for sharing user information with advertisers and government agencies despite promises that they wouldn't. This type of action generally gets shrugged off by the media and even by government officials. Facebook, as we write this, continues to be a powerful medium for social connections and sharing information on the world stage. The reality is that it isn't just "bad actors" who are purposely violating privacy. In fact, we read about privacy violations so frequently in the news that it seems we are becoming desensitized to it.

Our call to action in cybersecurity is to protect and serve. We are here to guard the vulnerable, and that means we are to protect their privacy.

An Outrageous Example of the Problem

We recently heard a story about privacy that speaks to the urgency of what we are facing, and we think it might be helpful for those in leadership. Our lawyer friend Jim walked into his law office building one day with his co-worker Gary. As they entered the lobby, they stopped to see a group of employees, from executive admins to clerks to partners, milling around and gawking at large printed images of emails, financial records, and personal photos that had been carefully placed on display near the company elevators in the most public walkway of the building. The firm employed 1,500 people in the four-story building, and everyone who came and went throughout the day had to pass through this main hallway. As Jim looked closer, he noticed a woman's name all over the information—it seemed familiar, but he just couldn't place it. Ironically, a security guard was standing in front of the wall and informing employees not to touch the display. He shrugged at Gary as they entered the elevator to head up to the office for their 9 a.m. conference call. Whatever was happening in that hallway was going to be quite embarrassing for someone.

As the two walked together into an "emergency" management meeting later that day, everyone in the company was buzzing about what had happened. The meeting was apparently going to address the morning's event, and as you can imagine, with a room full of legal experts, concern was high. Jim and Gary expected that the firm's partners had already responded with the proper protocols for whatever was transpiring. They wondered if the firm had been hacked or if this was some type of strange, isolated incident. Who was this employee whose emails and personal information had been posted in the lobby? Someone sitting behind them mentioned that even her Social Security and credit card numbers were on display. It was definitely stranger than fiction.

The explanation came quickly as a cybersecurity consultant walked into the front of the large conference room along with the CEO of the law firm. The specialist, Sheila, stood at the front of the room and clicked on a presentation that had the exact photos from the morning. She smiled calmly and said, "You probably noticed Jenna's private digital life was placed in the high-traffic lobby of the firm. It was displayed prominently so that everyone could see it. I am sure Jenna is devastated. I am sure she is horrified that her medical information, credit card numbers, Social Security number, home address, and even some of her very personal photos have been shared with everyone here at the firm today."

There was some murmuring around the room as the speaker paused. "Fortunately," she continued, "Jenna is *not* a real employee, and none of the information on display in the foyer hallway is real." This drew laughter from the large crowd of attorneys and law clerks. Sheila continued, "But, this should be a lesson for us. Every day, the private digital life of many of our clients is invaded and shared publicly. Sometimes, we even violate their privacy. Whenever you think about the invasion of privacy happening in the world of the Internet today, I want you to remember poor Jenna. It should inform how we defend our clients' privacy and how we protect our own digital lives."

We are told that this outlandish illustration had a lasting impact on Jim and the other attorneys at the firm. It is a poignant example of what we are facing across industries today. It is a call to arms for those in cybersecurity.

Remember: We Are the Shield

Protecting others from the perils of bad actors on the Internet is at the core of our mission. Whenever you question the urgency of this issue, just put yourself or any of your loved ones in Jenna's shoes. Would you want your personal information shared in the main walkways of your office every day? It is happening. An invasion of privacy far worse is being inflicted upon people you know as you read these lines. Protecting others has always been the primary responsibility of cybersecurity professionals. Whether you are working for a large corporation, at a government agency, or in an individual capacity, helping others become better educated about online activity is at the core of our cybersecurity role. Protecting the privacy and dignity of every human being is the aim of that endeavor. After all, we work in a human business.

   We are the shield that defends not just the data, finances, and healthcare of people—we are the ones who protect some of their basic human rights. Let that sink in for a moment. Privacy is connected to the very essence of what it means to be a free human being. If you work in a start-up, in a medical organization, or even a social media platform, you must be accountable to this principle of privacy. The invasion of privacy is so commonplace that we are becoming desensitized to the violation of a basic human right. There is never an excuse for a cybersecurity professional to take part in such activities or even be complicit. There is no profit margin, no competitive advantage, and no financial gain that should ever supersede our fundamental responsibility to protect the privacy, which is a fundamental human right, of others. As leaders and practitioners, we are to be unequivocal about our expectations in this area. While we know that "curiosity killed the cat" and our yearning to know things is often an essential quality that drives us to be great at our jobs, it must be harnessed and directed in the right way—with integrity and accountability. We encourage you to be clear and consistent with what you believe and allow those beliefs to dictate your actions.

Code-Critical Application

Read the following case study and answer the questions applying what you have learned in this chapter.

Case Study: To Share or Not to Share? Investigating the CFO's System

Karen and Chad have led the cybersecurity department at the regional hospital facility for nearly 10 years now. They have a great level of comfort working together and even get together with their spouses and children outside of the office quite frequently. They both report to the chief information officer (CIO) of the hospital and split the management duties of a strong cyber team that they have been instrumental in building since the pandemic. They are also on the front lines of innovation in healthcare security and have turned down other job offers because their families love the coastal city where they reside. Frankly, they enjoy their jobs because they work so well together managing the many security crises that come and go like the nearby ocean waves.

One day, a junior analyst happens to bring a potential breach into their stand-up afternoon security team meeting. The issue seems to involve several members of the executive team, and their policies and procedures are clear that either Karen or Chad should be present when investigating this type of situation. Karen has an off-site meeting that afternoon with a security vendor that the hospital may contract with in the next calendar year, so she agrees to let Chad be the manager present. Chad picks up the phone and informs the chief executive officer (CEO) that they will be looking through some sensitive information and that he will follow standard company policies and procedures.

The breach has the potential to be high-risk, so the CEO gives Chad permission to move forward quickly.

Chad begins to investigate the breach and traces it back to the chief financial officer's (CFO's) system. It appears to be a break-in through a mobile accounting application that the department is using, but he needs to take a closer look to see if any files were compromised. As Chad is looking through the CFO's system, he accidentally discovers a listing titled "Force Reduction," and before he can close out the file, he happens to notice his good friend and co-worker Karen's name at the very top of the list of suggested layoffs.

As he continues to investigate the breach, he realizes it is easily contained, but he also can't help himself. He circles back to the "Force Reduction" file one more time and looks more closely. Sure enough, it is a list for the CEO of employees who will be laid off at the end of the fiscal year. They are a month away, and Chad realizes that his friend Karen has no idea. In fact, Chad and Karen were both promised raises in the new fiscal year, both received great reviews, and Karen was even promised additional funds for staffing. Karen and her husband are about to close on a new house near the beach at the end of the week. On top of everything, Karen's husband has just given his company notice that he is leaving his lucrative sales position to launch a small business in the new year. Chad realizes that things couldn't line up any worse for his friend.

Karen returns from her meeting with the vendor that afternoon excited about the future of security at the hospital. She wants to tell Chad all about her meeting and asks him about the breach. Chad tells her that two of their top analysts are tying up the report and that they will review it tomorrow, but as he talks with his friend, he just can't "unsee" the force reduction information he found on CFO's system. He goes home that night and discusses this dilemma with his wife. Should he tell Karen? They have worked together for a decade, and he doesn't feel that it is ethically right for the company to lay her off right before the holidays. In fact, Chad feels like Karen has been lied to by their superiors. He is well aware that layoffs are happening everywhere in the industry, but could Karen get a new job? Very likely, she would, but she would also have to move out of the city to find a great position. Chad doesn't sleep well that evening, trying to decide the most ethical way to move forward, considering the information he has about his friend and co-worker's future.

Critical Application Questions

Is it ethical for the company to have promised Karen a raise and even discussed increasing her staff budget while later planning to lay her off in a force reduction move? How can we be sure that the list represents the final decision about lay-offs?

Does Chad have an ethical responsibility to tell Karen she is on the layoff list? If it is unethical, how would you sort out the challenge of seeing this information and not sharing it with a close friend?

Did Chad do anything wrong by seeing the "Force Reduction" file as he worked on the CFO's system?

(continued)

(*continues*)

How would you handle this situation if you were Chad?

Are there other avenues to approach this situation other than informing Karen that she is on the layoff list?

Could Chad approach the CIO about this dilemma?

Is Chad committing an ethical violation if he tells his wife? Or if he tells Karen?

How is this entire scenario informed by our commitment to protecting privacy?

Appendix A: The Cybersecurity Code of Honor

The challenge we have set before all of us, for those in the trenches all the way to the executive offices, is a big ask. Many leaders and policymakers consider cybersecurity to be the economic and security threat of our age. The stakes are high. It is one thing to write a code of honor and a cybersecurity ethics book, but executing these principles is a completely different matter. Our life experiences and professions serve as daily reminders of this difference and the importance of practicing our principles in the real world. However, let us assure you that we are far enough along the journey to champion the worthiness of such an endeavor and all that it will require. As we have said before, the benefits are far-reaching—corporately, professionally, and personally. Someone once said, "Right isn't always easy, but it is always right."

It is hard enough to teach, train, and practice a high ethical standard, but it is further compounded by situations where the ethical response is not always clear. The real-life, painstaking examples we have explored in this book give us a glimpse into those complexities. And not to pile on, but the complex realities of our world do not always serve us well. Culturally, many have been indoctrinated to respond based solely upon how they feel. Of course, there is nothing wrong with being aware of our emotions, but not to the exclusion of additional vitally important concerns about others and the impacts of our decisions on them. In reality, this means we may not be as practiced as we should be when making hard decisions. We must not succumb to our shortcomings and pressure. Yes, there will be days when the burden seems heavy, maybe even too heavy, but this is when we need to remember the words of tennis legend Billie Jean King, "Pressure is a privilege."

The Cybersecurity Code of Honor gives us the ability to withstand such pressure and, as a framework, gives the C-suite and those who are in the trenches every day a fighting chance. It requires that we focus and be mindful of those ideals that are fundamental (respect, protect, and serve others), be accountable, learn from mistakes, work collaboratively (no lone wolves), and practice discipline and self-control. Until the perfect human comes along, we need one another as well as the help of the Cybersecurity Code of Honor. The black hats are smart and out for all that benefits them, but we are better than that. We truly hope that the ethical standards discussed here and embodied in committing to the code of honor will encourage you to aspire for wisdom, the strength of will to set aside passing feelings, and the development of character that is rooted in a meaningful ethic.

When judges are sworn onto the bench, doctors commit to the Hippocratic oath, and witnesses raise their right hand and promise to tell the truth, the gravity of individual responsibility is brought to the forefront. Throughout history, civilized nations have cloaked oath-taking in ceremonial traditions, underscoring the significance of the commitment being made because it is calling forth the best from us. Oaths or code of honors should elicit humility and soberness for the responsibility, for the pressure, and for the privilege to which we are enlisting. When we sign the Cybersecurity Code of Honor, we are joining a broader collective that says our jobs matter, our work is valuable, and our industry's integrity is important and worth protecting. Let's band together and commit to the Cybersecurity Code of Honor that is as much about our integrity as it is about the dignity we see in the people who place their trust in us: "I solemnly swear to uphold to the best of my ability and judgment, in all my professional duties, personal practices, and future endeavors. . . ."

CYBERSECURITY CODE

I _____ solemnly swear to uphold to the best of my ability and judgment, in all my professional duties, personal practices, and future endeavors, the tenets of this pledge:

I will treat all people with dignity and respect.

I will seek the best interests of others.

I will strive to recognize, take ownership, and appropriately communicate my mistakes and exercise patience toward others who make errors.

I will be honest, trustworthy, and above reproach in my actions and communications.

I will not be a lone wolf, but will instead work collaboratively with my peers and superiors.

I will endeavor to exercise patience, wisdom, and self-control in all situations.

I will not steal and will do everything in my power to prevent theft in all its forms.

I will protect and respect the privacy of others.

Signed: _____ Date: _____

MONTREAT
COLLEGE

The creation of this code was sponsored by the National Centers of Academic Excellence in Cybersecurity in partnership with Montreat College, a private liberal arts college in North Carolina. Montreat College is recognized by the NSA as a Center of Academic Excellence in Cyber Defense.

Appendix B: Where Do We Go from Here?

Thank you for reading this book. Here are some next steps for adopting the Cybersecurity Code of Honor:

1. Individuals should sign the Cybersecurity Code of Honor included in Appendix A.

2. Everyone in a cyber department should sign the Code of Honor.

3. Companies should incorporate the Code of Honor into the company culture and make it part of the hiring process.

4. Educational institutions should encourage students to sign the Code of Honor as a rite of passage into the cybersecurity world.

5. Institutions and corporations should consider creating a tradition or a ceremony of sorts to further communicate the importance of this Code of Honor. If committing to the Code of Honor is primarily an individual function, e.g., a required step in the hiring process, you

can consider giving a special pen for the signing. The pen becomes a welcome gift from the company and a symbol of the individual's commitment.

6. Visit our website at www.montreat.edu/cyber-oath to download, personalize, and print a frame-worthy copy of the Cybersecurity Code of Honor.

Notes

Chapter 1

1. https://aag-it.com/the-latest-2022-cyber-crime-statistics
2. https://ascendantusa.com/2022/05/14/cost-of-cyber-attacks-on-business-in-2022
3. https://aag-it.com/the-latest-2022-cyber-crime-statistics
4. www.medicinenet.com/hippocratic_oath/definition.htm

Chapter 2

5. https://webhome.auburn.edu/~vestmon/robotics.html

Chapter 3

6. https://cybersecurityventures.com/cybersecurity-spending-2021-2025
7. www.forbes.com/sites/rodgerdeanduncan/2018/09/11/the-why-of-work-purpose-and-meaning-really-do-matter/?sh=45267ff068e1
8. https://hbr.org/2019/07/to-be-happier-at-work-invest-more-in-your-relationships
9. www.indeed.com/career-advice/career-development/how-to-improve-emotional-intelligence
10. www.zdnet.com/article/retailers-to-share-threat-data-in-cybersecurity-powwow

Chapter 4

11. www.theregister.com/2022/03/28/okta_lapsuss_faq_
    admits_mistake

Chapter 5

12. https://greatergood.berkeley.edu/article/item/
    john_gottman_on_trust_and_betrayal

Chapter 7

13. www.insider.com/photos-titanic-passengers-getting-
    rescued-by-carpathia-2020-4#there-were-not-enough-
    lifeboats-to-hold-the-number-f-passengers-that-
    needed-to-evacuate-and-the-titanics-officers-
    and-crew-were-not-trained-as-a-team-in-the-
    handling-of-lifeboats-5

Chapter 8

14. www.forbes.com/sites/edwardsegal/2020/
    12/14how-to-guard-against-corporate-credit-card-
    and-expense-report-fraud/?sh=466b83eef85f
15. https://leftronic.com/blog/employee-theft-
    statistics
16. http://mythfolklore.blogspot.com/2014/06/
    blackfoot-theft-from-sun.html

Chapter 9

17. www.remindercall.com/blog/celebrity-hipaa-
    fails
18. www.nbcnews.com/tech/social-media/timeline-facebook-
    s-privacy-issues-its-responses-n859651
19. www.ftc.gov/news-events/news/press-releases/
    2019/07/ftc-imposes-5-billion-penalty-sweeping-
    new-privacy-restrictions-facebook
20. www.washingtonpost.com/technology/2021/08/29/facebook-
    privacy-monopoly

Acknowledgments

From Paul J. Maurer:

This book would not be possible without the love and support of my wife, Joellen, over these past decades. She has always given me the freedom and encouragement to dream big and reach high.

Regarding this project, I want to express my deep gratitude to and for Lynne Clark. Lynne's thinking on the matter of cybersecurity ethics is seminal. Because Lynne's leadership role at the National Security Agency places her in a position of great influence over the development of the nation's cybersecurity professionals, that seminal thinking has significant national security implications. Lynne recognized the need for the next generation of cybersecurity students and professionals to have an ethical framework at the heart of the high-stakes, fast-paced decisions these folks make every day to protect the people of our nation against cyber-attacks. I am grateful and honored that she asked Montreat College to lead the way in creating this work. I sincerely hope it fulfills her and the agency's aims for the next generation of cybersecurity professionals.

I am grateful beyond words for my co-author, Ed Skoudis. He was truly the perfect partner for this book. His experience and expertise in cybersecurity is exceptional. The case studies and practical application are the product of Ed's experience and wisdom, gleaned from his deep knowledge of many of the major cybersecurity breaches in the U.S. over the past two-plus decades. But beyond his knowledge and wisdom, Ed is a classic gentleman, a gracious collaborator, and a true friend.

Matt Litton worked closely with Ed and me to figure out how to put our thinking and content into writing and create a structure that makes sense. When others doubted its centrality, he was a persuasive champion for the cybersecurity oath as the centerpiece. Matt's manuscript provided a tremendous foundation from which to refine our thinking as we edited. It's hard to imagine doing this without Matt.

I'm also grateful for the team of collaborators over the past few years who provided feedback and wisdom as the project came into shape. They served as valued advisors. This team includes Kelli Burgin, John Gallagher, Sandy Shugart, Rodney Peterson, Crosland Stuart, and David Thompson. Last but not least, I'm thankful for Zlata Kolesnyk, my student worker at Montreat College who assisted with various parts of the project.

From Ed Skoudis:

To the Four Js—I love you all so much, I have no words.

To my parents and Nana—You have always supported and encouraged me to do the right thing unapologetically. Thank you.

To my amazing Counter Hack team—I'm so grateful to each and every one of you. Thank you for your trust in me.

To all of the incredible SANS Students, Instructors, and Authors I've had the honor of working with—Your stories, struggles, and triumphs have inspired so much of what I was able to bring to this book. I am profoundly grateful for all you've shared with me over the past quarter century.

To the SANS Institute team—You all have defined me, inspired me, taken care of me, and blessed me in countless ways. I'm so grateful for you all!

To the SANS.edu team—You are changing lives profoundly, and I'm honored to help serve your mission.

To my co-author, Paul—This book was all your idea. I appreciate the invitation to be a part of it, and I am profoundly grateful for you. Your steady, creative, and strong leadership of Montreat College is an inspiration to me and so many others. Thank you for your friendship and tireless motivation!

To Lynne Clark—You were absolutely instrumental in inspiring this book with your sharp focus on the importance of character and ethics in the cybersecurity community.

To Matt Litton—Thank you for wielding your writing pen with excellence in capturing ideas over which Paul and I wrestled for so long. You helped organize them and bring them to life on the page, my friend.

To the wonderful "book people" working on this tome—Crosland Stuart, Jim Minatel, and all the other great people at Wiley & Sons—You are true pros and a delight to work with. . . . er. . . with whom to work.

About the Authors

Paul J. Maurer has served as president & CEO of Montreat College since 2014 and has served in higher education for the past 25 years. Montreat College is recognized at the highest levels of the United States government as a national leader in cybersecurity education and workforce development. Montreat gained designation as a Center of Academic Excellence (CAE) by the National Security Agency (NSA) in 2017.

Dr. Maurer is a frequent speaker on a variety of topics. He earned his Ph.D. in political science from Claremont Graduate University, where he was an H. B. Earhart Fellow and a John M. Olin Fellow. He earned his Master of Divinity from Gordon-Conwell Theological Seminary and his B.A. from the University of Cincinnati, where he was co-captain of the men's soccer team. He has a special talent for cutting his own hair. Dr. Maurer and his wife, Joellen, have been married since 1989 and have four children, a daughter-in-law, and three grandchildren.

Ed Skoudis has taught over 40,000 security professionals globally in penetration testing, incident handling, and cybersecurity professionalism. Ed currently serves as the President of the SANS Technology Institute college, supporting over 2,000 current students earning their master's degrees, bachelor's degrees, and cyber security certificates. Additionally, Ed is one of the first authorities consistently brought in to provide post-attack analysis of major breach cases. Ed is also the founder of the SANS Penetration Testing Curriculum, the CEO and founder of the Counter Hack consulting firm, and the leader of the team that builds SANS NetWars and the SANS Holiday Hack Challenge. He was honored to receive the Order of Thor recognition for his contributions to the community of military cyber professionals. Ed is a keynote speaker and an Advisory Board member for the RSA Conference, the largest gathering of cybersecurity professionals in the world. He is also on the board of directors for Manasquan Bank and a charity.

Index